"Robust, accessi[...] By the Way pain[...] way. This is a bo[...] tion to read."

"Like a splash of water to the face, *By the Way* awakens us to the realities of discipleship offered via the way of the cross, the kingdom, the resurrection, and of course the life and reign of Jesus. After reading it, we walk away not with a new to-do list but with a new way of life in his presence. Winsome, story-filled, theologically sound. In writing this book, Vreeland is pastoring us to a deeper Christian life."

"For too long, approaches to discipleship have been focused on a set of affirmations or a body of information rather than a pattern of living. Derek Vreeland sets out here to change that. With clarity and accessibility, Vreeland lays out a map of the many contours of the Jesus way, complete with practices and reflections. This book will help us become better followers of Jesus and better at inviting others to do the same."

"For far too long, many in the church have equated faith as a one-time decision we make rather than an ongoing way we take. This fundamental misreading of Jesus' invitation to salvation has resulted in stunted growth, anemic witness, and a profound lack of God's life flowing through our lives. This is why we need to listen to Derek Vreeland. *By the Way* offers us a fresh vision of what it means to say yes to Jesus' way, which immerses us in truth and invigorates us with life."

"I know this book will grip your heart. You are going to fall deeper in love with Jesus, his church, and people who have yet to taste and see that the Lord is so good. . . . Through the pages of this book, Derek Vreeland is going to help you reimagine what it means to follow Jesus."

—**Derwin L. Gray**, lead pastor of Transformation Church and author of *Limitless Life*, from foreword

"This book is a breath of fresh air! Following Jesus is indeed a loving way of life. We do not follow Jesus in our minds alone or by having 'right' doctrine alone. That is modern-day gnosticism. It would behoove those of us serious about living out the gospel to pay attention and to learn—or perhaps relearn—from Derek Vreeland."

—**Marlena Graves**, author of *A Beautiful Disaster*

"I love Derek Vreeland and I love books on discipleship, so reading a book by Derek Vreeland about discipleship is a dream come true! Thank you, Derek, for capturing the beauty of the way of Jesus in this practical and compelling guidebook. *By the Way* shows us how a life of radical allegiance to Jesus is not only possible, but the only way to really live."

—**Bruxy Cavey**, author of *Reunion* and senior pastor of The Meeting House

"Salvation sold cheap, as a ticket to heaven, bears little resemblance to what Jesus and the apostles proclaimed as a robust way of life. *By the Way* is an important and timely book: a book written by an experienced pastor seeking to close the embarrassing gap between what is glibly called 'salvation' and the way of discipleship to which Jesus actually calls us. *By the Way* will help many people discover the way that leads to life."

—**Brian Zahnd**, lead pastor of Word of Life Church and author of *Postcards from Babylon* btw

by the way

Getting Serious
about Following Jesus

Derek Vreeland

HERALD
P R E S S

Harrisonburg, Virginia

Herald Press
PO Box 866, Harrisonburg, Virginia 22803
www.HeraldPress.com

Library of Congress Cataloging-in-Publication Data
Names: Vreeland, Derek, author.
Title: By the way : getting serious about following Jesus / Derek Vreeland.
Description: Harrisonburg : Herald Press, 2019.
Identifiers: LCCN 2018060613| ISBN 9781513805863 (pbk. : alk. paper) | ISBN
   9781513805870 (hardcover : alk. paper)
Subjects: LCSH: Spiritual formation.
Classification: LCC BV4511 .V74 2019 | DDC 248.4--dc23 LC record available
at https://lccn.loc.gov/2018060613

BY THE WAY
© 2019 by Herald Press, Harrisonburg, Virginia 22803. 800-245-7894.
   All rights reserved.
Library of Congress Control Number: 2018060613
International Standard Book Number: 978-1-5138-0586-3 (paperback);
   978-1-5138-0587-0 (hardcover); 978-1-5138-0588-7 (ebook)
Printed in United States of America
Cover and interior design by Reuben Graham

Unless otherwise noted, Scripture quotations are from the ESV® Bible (*The Holy
Bible, English Standard Version*®), © 2001 by Crossway, a publishing ministry of
Good News Publishers. Used by permission. All rights reserved.

Scripture taken from *The Message.* © 1993, 1994, 1995, 1996, 2000, 2001, 2002.
Used by permission of NavPress Publishing Group.

23 22 21 20 19   10 9 8 7 6 5 4 3 2 1

To Jenni—
who, by the way, has been with me every step of the way

I remember thee upon my bed, and meditate on thee in the night watches. Because thou hast been my help, therefore in the shadow of thy wings will I rejoice. My soul followeth hard after thee.

—Psalm 63:6-8 KJV

Contents

Foreword

J esus saves us so that through us he can save the world."
My friend Derek Vreeland writes these beautiful words in
chapter 1. These words are beautiful because they are true.
My heart was gripped when I first laid eyes on them, just as
I know this book will grip your heart too. You are going to
fall deeper in love with Jesus, his church, his mission for his
church, and people who have yet to taste and see that the
Lord is so good.

How amazing is it that Jesus shares his eternal-kind-of-life,
ministry, and mission with his disciples? It's mind-blowing to
contemplate that Jesus right now is seated at the right hand of
his Father, in a realm that the New Testament calls heaven, yet
Jesus expresses himself on earth through his disciples, called
the body of Christ (1 Corinthians 12:27). Jesus loves, for-
gives, and transforms, and brings glimpses of heaven to earth

through his people. Through the pages of this book, Derek will help you reimagine what it means to follow Jesus.

Like a skilled guide, he will reveal to you how consumerism and Western individualism have negatively shaped your faith. Consumerism tells a story that Jesus and his church are a product that exists to meet your needs. It's as if Jesus is a wonderfully trained Chick-fil-A employee whose pleasure it is to make sure your order is to your liking.

In Western individualism, instead of placing Jesus and his church as the focus of your faith, you, the individual, become the focus. Often, the church in North America has transformed the gospel from a corporate, communal understanding to an individualistic, private faith. The gospel becomes a story of how Jesus came to save me from the wrath of God and to help me reach heaven when I die, instead of a story of God in Christ rescuing, reconciling, and redeeming a people who exist for the glory and mission of God, displaying a foretaste of God's kingdom on earth as conduits of love (1 Peter 2:9).

Let this marinate for a moment: The New Testament authors use the word *disciple* over 260 times and the word *Christian* only 3 times to describe Jesus' followers. The term *Christian* describes how Jews and Gentiles became a new, multiethnic family. In the early church, Jews began to worship Jesus of Nazareth as YHWH (or Yahweh) and Gentiles stopped worshiping idols and starting worshiping Jesus. It's as though they became a new ethnicity on earth comprised of all ethnicities united in and by the blood of Jesus in fulfillment of God's covenant with Abraham (Genesis 12:1-3; Ephesians 2:8-16). The Scripture says, "The disciples were first called Christians at Antioch" (Acts 11:26 CSB). Unfortunately, the term *Christian* has lost its meaning.

A disciple is an apprentice of Jesus, in the community (church) of Jesus, who relies on the life of Jesus through the Holy Spirit's presence and power to reproduce Jesus' life, ministry, and mission. God is calling you to so much more. God is calling you to a new way to be human, to be enlightened by God's gospel-truth, and to live by the power of Jesus' very life.

—Dr. Derwin L. Gray
Lead pastor of Transformation Church and author of *The High-Definition Leader: Building Multiethnic Churches in a Multiethnic World*

Introduction

On a lazy summer Sunday afternoon, my wife and I sat poolside talking about the day, and the seeds of this book began to germinate in my mind. When I told her I wanted to write a book for discipleship, she asked me, "And what exactly is that?"

"Discipleship? It's about following Jesus," I answered. "Living a certain kind of life that identifies with Jesus in his death and resurrection."

Not satisfied with a simple definition, she pressed further. "And what does that look like in real life?"

"Don't lie. Tell the truth. Don't kill people. Don't cheat on your spouse. Be kind and respectful," were the first things that came to mind.

She didn't hesitate. "Everybody knows to do those things. Every good mom, Christian or not, raises her child to tell the truth, not to hurt people, and to be kind. What makes following Jesus so special?"

At first I protested, "People accept those cultural values because Western civilization has been shaped by Jesus whether they realize it or not. The value of human life is one of the great triumphs of the gospel. Ancient Romans gave little respect to slaves, women, or children. The respect for human dignity comes to us because of Jesus. But if I'm honest, Western civilization, particularly the American experiment, has equally been influenced by classical Greek thought with an emphasis on intellectual and moral virtue."

I stopped talking for a moment. I realized I hadn't really answered her question: *What makes following Jesus unique?* What a great question! I hope this book answers it.

I agree with Stanley Hauerwas's insistence that our lives as followers of Jesus should look foolish, even meaningless, if Jesus isn't the way, truth, and life. He writes, "For I take it to be crucial that Christians must live in such a manner that their lives are unintelligible if the God we worship in Jesus Christ does not exist."[1] Believing in Jesus and following Jesus in a world where Christians no longer have the most influential voice in cultural discussions requires the kind of Christian life where people are serious about discipleship.

In his classic work *The Divine Conspiracy*, Dallas Willard notes that the lack of making disciples continues to haunt the church. He observers, "Nondiscipleship is the elephant in the church. It is not the much-discussed moral failures, financial abuses, or the amazing general similarity between Christians and non-Christians. These are only effects of the underlying problem."[2]

I can no longer accept that reality. I can't rest knowing that we in the church are producing good people, educated people, "Spirit-filled" people, but not people who live distinct lives shaped by the cross and resurrection. This book is my humble attempt to change that trend.

This book isn't *about* discipleship. It's a book *for* discipleship. It's a guide for those who want to grow as disciples of Jesus. It's a way of thinking about the various ways we live as followers of Jesus. Each of these ways is rooted in what we think about the God revealed in Jesus Christ and made known by the Holy Spirit; that is to say, these ways each have a theological foundation. The way of the gospel, the cross, and resurrection in chapters 2–4 roots our lives of discipleship in the fundamental message of the Christian faith. Chapter 5 discusses the way of love as defined by the Trinity. God is love and the trajectory of our lives depends on how we respond to that love. Upon this foundation of love we will explore the necessity of critical thinking and character formation in chapters 6 and 7. Following Jesus is not all about a change of mind or a change of heart, but both. Chapters 8 and 9 describe our participation in the life of the church and the habits we keep that in turn form us into disciples. We bring our discipleship journey to an end in chapter 10 by renewing our understanding of God's mission in terms of justice, participating with God in the work of setting right a world gone wrong. These ways of living find a balance between the cross and the resurrection, love and justice, critical thinking and spiritual formation, inward habits and community practices.

I am grateful for so many people who have made this book possible. I am thinking specifically of Barry Reynolds, my coach and English teacher who encouraged me to write from a Christian perspective as a follower of Jesus in a public high school. I'm especially grateful to have reconnected with Barry as an adult before his untimely death in 2017. Many of my seminary professors encouraged me to think and write theologically. Thank you in particular to Henry Lederle and David Dorries. Thanks also to Darrell Chatraw for loving me like a son and treating me like a colleague. Your pastoral heart and love for people and teaching is for me a living reminder of Jesus. I'm indebted to Steve Seamands at Asbury Theological Seminary for awakening me to the centrality of the Trinity in ministry and church life. Thank you for encouraging me to write boldly to my tribe. Thanks to Tom Wright, my theological mentor from afar. Your theological convictions have been nothing short of revolutionary for me. Thanks for encouraging me to say what I have to say in my own voice. I'm also the recipient of so much grace through the writings of the late Eugene Peterson. It isn't an exaggeration to say that Eugene Peterson saved my life as a pastor. May God's grace enable me to carry on Eugene's gentle, kind, pastoral wisdom.

A huge thank you to the two wonderful churches I have served as a pastor, Cornerstone Church in Americus, Georgia, and Word of Life Church in St. Joseph, Missouri. I love these congregations with all my heart. Thanks for loving me and supporting me in pursuing God's call for me to teach, write, and be a voice. I'm particularly grateful for Brian Zahnd, my pastor, my boss, and my friend. Thank you for remaining courageously faithful to the Christ of perpetual surprise. Apologies in advance for anything I learned from you and did not directly attribute to you in this book. No one has shaped my theological imagination more than you. I'm glad we get to do life and ministry together. You know I'll be with you when the deal goes down.

Thanks are also in order to my parents and my brother Jeff who have been never-ending sources of support. Speaking of encouragement, thanks to my many pastor friends and fellow Jesus-followers who have inspired and encouraged me. Cassidy Kipple, Sarah Zahnd, and Melissa Medsker each took time to read my manuscript and provide helpful feedback in shaping the final draft. Thank you, friends, for your helpful comments. I appreciate Matthew Rose, Steve Dunmire, and Joey Jennings for hosting me at the Refresh Retreat and Family Camp at Houghton College in western New York in the summer of 2017. You asked me to speak on discipleship. My nightly sermons that week became the seeds for this book. I wrote the first draft of chapter 1 during my down time while on Houghton's beautiful campus.

Most of all, thank you to my family—Jenni, Wesley, Maggie, Taylor, and Dylan. I love each of you with all my heart. Thank you for loving me, for giving me space to write, for extending grace to me when I get grumpy, and for going along with me on this journey of following Jesus. Lastly I am deeply indebted to Valerie Weaver-Zercher, Melodie Davis, Jodi Hertzler, and the wonderful team at Herald Press. Thank you for believing in my words and for working with such diligence to make the dream of this book a reality.

1

Disciple

The Way of Jesus

It all starts with baptism. I was baptized on Super Bowl Sunday, January 26, 1986, when Mike Ditka's Chicago Bears destroyed the New England Patriots with a dominating defense. This was the Super Bowl marked by the "Super Bowl Shuffle," Jim McMahon's headbands, William "Refrigerator" Perry, and one of the best NFL defenses of the 1980s. While everyone not living in the Boston area was celebrating the Bears' Super Bowl victory, I was starting a new life in Christ as an eleven-year-old son of the South living in the Midwest. I remember hearing the gospel preached at my Baptist church as I sat with my family on those unforgiving pews. My desire to become a Christian and be baptized wasn't merely to do the right thing; I wanted to follow Jesus. As I entered into the awkward season of early adolescence, I became a "space cadet," lost in my own thoughts as I tried to navigate life amid the wild changes associated with one's middle school years. I had been baptized. I had taken my first steps in following in the footsteps of Jesus. But with adolescence things had changed. Participation in the life of our church slowly began to fall away, as did my pursuit of Jesus. Then, when I was fifteen years old, Jesus met me in the wilderness of my perpetual insecurity. With this surprising encounter with Jesus, everything began to change.

In those three years between baptism and my encounter with Jesus, my church attendance was off and on—by the time I entered high school, it was mostly off. I was well on my way to becoming just another in-name-only Christian. My mom remained the faithful churchgoer of the family. She often asked me to go with her, but I quickly learned the trick of hiding under the covers in my bed, pretending to be asleep, periodically poking my head out to check the clock. I knew if I stayed in bed beyond a certain point of time, there simply would not be enough time to get ready for church. My trick worked most of the time and my mom was never really pushy about it. I do have memories of her consistency in Sunday morning worship. She set an example I was soon to follow.

During my sophomore year of high school my dad decided that the entire family was going back to church. His surge of faith led to my own. My dad grew up in a military home as an Air Force brat. Subsequently he served in the military right out of high school. I grew up knowing that when Dad said the family was doing something, the proper response was to click our heels together, salute, and say, "Yes, sir." Disappointment ran through me like ice cold water when I heard his pronouncement about church. The last thing I wanted to do on Sunday morning was to go to church. Cheerios and

MTV had become my Sunday morning liturgy. With the TV remote in one hand and a spoon in the other, I would put my troubled teenage mind to rest with a simple bowl of cereal and pop stars parading around like musicians, lip-syncing their songs on television. Those days were over. We were going back to church.

I reluctantly walked with my family from the parking lot to the rear doors of the church on our first Sunday back. The building seemed familiar. But the people gathered around the door looked like strangers. We had arrived early to catch a Sunday school class before the worship service started. My parents introduced my brother and me to the smiling strangers at the door. I stared at my feet as I heard the woman at the door say, "The youth meet for Sunday school right down this hall." I nervously looked up and saw a rather attractive girl near my age walking toward me. Apparently she had been summoned to escort me down the hall to the Sunday school classroom. She had big, permed, 80s-looking blond hair, and she smiled while she talked. She told me about their youth group, the youth pastor, and their Sunday school class as she led me into the nondescript room full of noisy teenagers clustered in rows of metal folding chairs. I found a seat in the back conveniently positioned in an empty row. Outside of my friendly female usher, I remember nothing else about the Sunday school class except for Michael Gaines, a tall, lanky guy a few years older than me who talked to me about basketball. As a fifteen-year-old in the age of Air Jordan, basketball was my life. Michael leaned over the back of his folding chair and introduced himself and surprisingly asked me who I was and what I was interested in. When I mentioned basketball, we talked until the beginning of the class about teams we followed and players we admired. I remember thinking, "Maybe these church kids aren't so bad after all." Looking back, I don't remember the content of the Sunday school lesson. I don't remember the songs we sang in church. I don't remember anything about the service. But I do remember the kindness of Michael Gaines.

I proceeded to go to the weekly youth group meetings on Wednesday nights. One fateful spring day, I attended a youth rally held on a Friday night in the gym of our local regional university. I honestly went to play basketball and possibly— just maybe—have the chance to meet some girls. I came away with so much more. At the close of the event, our youth pastor had us gather on the hardwood gym floor near the volleyball net. There, in that seemingly common place, he preached the uncommon gospel of grace. He talked about Jesus' death and resurrection and Jesus' invitation for us to come and follow him. He made no appeals for us to ask Jesus into our hearts or to accept Christ so we could go to heaven when we die. Jesus had died and risen for our salvation. This was God's gift of grace. Our response was to offer God our lives, abandon every other way to life, and follow Jesus. He asked us a pointed and direct question: "If you died tonight would Jesus be happy to see you because he knew you or would he be surprised to see you because you didn't have a relationship with him?" I knew I wasn't following Jesus. As an adult looking back, I can see the unnecessary guilt underneath the surface of our youth pastor's appeal. I have come to discover that God's love for me, and indeed all of us, remains unchanged by human behavior. However, in that moment, as a teenager with little to no knowledge of God, I didn't think Jesus would be happy to see me. Our youth pastor offered to pray with students after the rally, but I was hesitant.

I drove home after the youth event sometime after midnight with my mind jumping from question to question. *Was I following Jesus? Did I know Jesus? Did I want to be a Christian? What would it mean to be a follower of Jesus? Was my life pleasing to God? Did I even know who God was? Was I willing to lay down my life to accept a new life with Jesus? What in my life would change? What needed to change? Was I willing to submit every thought, every plan, every desire, to God? What was I supposed to do now?* My heart had been stirred. My youth pastor's question had my mind racing. As I pulled up in the driveway at home, I honestly didn't know what to do next. Walking up the cement steps toward the front door of my house sparked an idea. Once inside, I found my dad's big black Bible. I took it upstairs to my bedroom, closed the door, sat down on my bed, and began flipping through the pages.

I hadn't been much of a Bible reader, so I didn't know my way around this sacred and complex book. I did what I now tell people never to do. After turning page after page to no avail, I closed it and took a deep breath. I opened it again and pointed to a verse. I have come to learn that this method only works once in a person's lifetime. As it turns out, this night was my once in a lifetime. The verse I read that night in the quietness of my bedroom changed everything. I read these words: "Commit your way to the Lord; trust in him, and he will act" (Psalm 37:5). I realized that even though I had been baptized, I hadn't committed my way to the Lord. I hadn't yet taken my baptismal identity seriously. I hadn't become an intentional follower of Jesus. Gripping that Bible in my hands, I prayed a simple prayer, committing my life to the way of Jesus. That night I took my first step as a baptized disciple.

FOLLOW ME

Jesus began his rescue mission with these words: "Repent: for the kingdom of heaven is at hand" (Matthew 4:17). His punchy one-line sermon would be the central theme of his preaching and teaching. Repent, rethink, and realign your life around this stunning announcement. God's kingdom—God's rule and reign on earth—is coming from heaven. When Jesus began his preaching ministry, God's people were living as exiles in their ancestral land. They were home, but their home was overrun with an unwelcome guest—the most powerful military force in the ancient world, the Roman Empire. The people of Israel were longing for the personal presence of God to come and dwell among them again. They were waiting for the King, the Messiah, to establish God's kingdom and expel the Romans.

Jesus alerted them that the time was now.

Immediately after his audacious announcement, Jesus went walking down the road. The next order of business was to initiate a conversation with two brothers, two ordinary fishermen. He caught them casting their fishing nets into the Sea of Galilee and his conversation was short. He called out to them, "Follow me, and I will make you fishers of men" (Matthew 4:19). He didn't elaborate or make false promises. He didn't make any promises other than to make them fishers of men. He didn't sell the brothers on the benefits of following him. He simply said, "Follow me."

Jesus went from city to city teaching in the Jewish synagogues, preaching the gospel of the kingdom, demonstrating the nature of God's kingdom by healing the sick. But he did more than preaching and healing. Jesus called people to follow him, to become apprentices of sorts by becoming his disciples. Apprentices do not learn from absorbing information from a book, as good and as helpful as books are; they learn by watching and imitating the master artisan they are following. The master-apprentice relationship follows a pattern similar to this:

1. The master does and the apprentice watches.
2. The master does and the apprentice helps. They work together.
3. The apprentice does and the master watches, helping the apprentice make course corrections when necessary.
4. The apprentice does on his or her own, checking in with the master when needed.

As followers of Jesus we are his apprentices, called to watch how he does things and to learn the way of life from him.

Jesus launched the kingdom of God and by his words and actions he demonstrated what living as kingdom citizens would look like. He called others to follow him. His rescue mission wasn't going to be a solo project. It would be carried on by his apprentices, his disciples. After Jesus was gone, the kingdom of God would be embodied by all those who said yes to his call to follow him. Some two millennia later, Jesus is still proclaiming and demonstrating the kingdom of God and Jesus is still sliding his invitation across the table to us. His invitation is as simple today as it always was. When we open the envelope and read the white card inside, it only has two words printed in a simple black font: Follow me.

A WAY OF LIFE

The invitation from Jesus is for us to *follow him* because Christianity is not primarily a set of beliefs, even though what we believe is massively important. It isn't primarily a personal

relationship with God, even if personal faith and responsibility are absolutely necessary. It isn't primarily a religion, even
though the liturgies that shape the worship and work of the
church are indispensable. Christianity is principally a way of
living shaped by the Holy Spirit around the death and resurrection of Jesus. It isn't theology, religion, or personal devotion
to God that most forms our identity as Christians. Rather, we
are most formed by the pattern of our lives in direct reflection
of the life of Jesus.

Evangelicals have inherited an allergic reaction from the
ghosts of the Reformation to anything that may sound like
earning our salvation.[1] The Protestant Reformers of the sixteenth century critiqued the Roman Catholic practice of sell-
ing indulgences (pardons) as a way to purchase the salvation
of a long-departed loved one. Salvation cannot be bought and
sold; salvation is offered as a free gift of grace. Justification
by grace through faith is true, and Protestants react against
the residual aftertaste of the resistance to anything that feels
like "works" (that is, those activities we do in order to garner God's attention in order to somehow earn our salvation).
While salvation is one way to describe Jesus' rescue mission to
save the world, we are not saved *by* works—we are saved *for*
works. Paul emphatically states that it is "by grace you have
been saved through faith. And this is not your own doing; it
is the gift of God, not a result of works" (Ephesians 2:8-9).
However, Paul does not stop there. He continues by adding,
"For we are his workmanship, created in Christ Jesus for good
works" (Ephesians 2:10). Jesus saves us so that through us he
can save the world. Jesus comes to free humanity, forgiving us
of our sins, and restoring us as God's image-bearing creatures
reflecting his beauty as revealed in Jesus. We reflect the image

of Jesus into the world like a mirror. Our mirrored reflection is constructed by the way we live made distinct by the life and work of Jesus and the Spirit.

The earliest name for the group of Jesus-followers was "the Way." As Paul offered a defense to the accusation that he was stirring up riots in Jewish communities, he testified, saying, "I confess to you, that according to the Way, which they call a sect, I worship the God of our fathers, believing everything laid down by the Law and written in the Prophets" (Acts 24:14). People of the Way were criticized for stirring up trouble, because they proclaimed as King the one whom Jewish leaders rejected as a false prophet. The beliefs of those of the Way remained fuzzy in the minds of both Jews and Gentiles. For Greek-minded Gentiles with their pursuit of wisdom and intellectual sophistication, the preaching of a crucified King was pure silliness. Significance for the Greeks and Romans was found in intellectual pursuits, power, and domination. They were likely thinking to themselves, "Who wants to follow a god who became mortal and talked about humility and becoming a servant?" For Jewish people the preaching of the followers of the Way was a stumbling block. They expected God to return to God's people and they expected the reign of Messiah to come and restore the kingdom to Israel, but the Messiah could not be God. That would be blasphemy. Furthermore, Jesus could not be the Messiah because he was crucified, and as all Israel knew, a crucified Messiah was a failed Messiah. The followers of the Way, however, came to discover that their belief in Christ crucified was infused with the power of God, the power to rescue and transform lives.

As the church began to expand and grow, its people were increasingly known not so much for what they believed, but for the way they lived. They were known for their radical hospitality and care for the poor and marginalized. Throughout the Roman Empire, citizens were permitted by law to discard unwanted newborn babies. The practice of exposure was culturally accepted in the Roman world, so if an unwanted child was born, the family could leave the child on the top of a trash heap where the child would die by exposure to the elements or by being eaten by wild animals. Today we shudder at the idea of anyone doing anything like that to a little baby. The reason that Christians and non-Christians in our modern world value the life of children is the great triumph of Christ and those who over the centuries have walked in his ways. Christians in the Roman Empire were known to rescue and adopt into their homes babies that had been left to die of exposure. Values prevalent in Western culture like adoption, education for all, and care for the sick, the poor, and the aged are all products of a culture influenced by followers of Jesus. The way of Jesus resounds with caring for the weakest and most vulnerable among us.

DUSTING OFF THE ABANDONED WAYS OF GOD

We tend to lose sight of the centrality of the Christian life as a practice, as a distinct way of living. Instead, we focus on getting our theology just right. We want our worship services to challenge us and form us in the Jesus way and still be attractive to our non-Christian friends. We want to know exactly how best to communicate the gospel in a post-Christian culture. All of these are noble and crucial pursuits in following Jesus. But they tend to cause us to overlook the essential nature of the Christian life, which is to live a life walking in the ways of Jesus. When we look back into our history as the people of God, we see this theme shining brightly.

One of the oldest Christian documents not included in the New Testament is called "The Didache," or "The Twelve." It opens with these lines: "There are two Ways: a Way of Life and a Way of Death, and the difference between these two Ways is great. The Way of Life is this: Thou shalt love first the Lord thy Creator, and secondly thy neighbour as thyself; and thou shalt do nothing to any man that thou wouldst not wish to be done to thyself."[2] The Didache seeks to provide us a summation of the apostles' teachings, and the opening reveals how the early church talked about the Christian faith. We find before us two ways, the way of Jesus leading to life and the way of sin leading to death. The way of life is the Jesus way, the way of living according to the dictates of love. For Christians the way of love isn't a mushy, fluttery-heart, sentimental kind of love, but love that serves and sacrifices for the sake of the other. In a world at war, people too often discard the way of love.

The Old Testament, particularly the Psalms, is filled with appeals for the people of God to walk in God's ways. The first psalm opens with "Blessed is the man who walks not in the counsel of the wicked nor stands in the way of sinners" (Psalm 1:1). The psalm writer contrasts "the way of sinners" with "the way of the righteous" (Psalm 1:6): those who delight and meditate on God's law and thus yield fruit. The Psalms contain a number of references to the ways of God.[3] Deeply embedded in this collection of Psalms is the spirit of the ancient people of God who were shaped by either the ways of life or the ways of death, depending on whether or not they walked in the ways of God.

In the New Testament, Paul writes to the church in Colossae, offering these words of encouragement: "Therefore, as you received Christ Jesus the Lord, so walk in him, rooted and built up in him and established in the faith, just as you were taught, abounding in thanksgiving" (Colossians 2:6-7). When we turn in faith to King Jesus, we receive him and enter into the kingdom of God through the waters of baptism. Once we receive Christ, Paul invites us to walk in him, because we don't simply receive Christ so we can add King Jesus to a collection of ideas we set on some mental shelf. We receive Christ so we can walk in his ways, developing roots deep in the rich soil of the historic faith. James echoes with similar words of encouragement when he writes, "But be doers of the word, and not hearers only" (James 1:22). Hearing is easy; implementing what we hear is the real work of following Jesus. We become doers of the word precisely because our faith is animated by the works we do.

DRAWN IRRESISTIBLY TO JESUS

Jesus closes the Sermon on the Mount with an illustration bringing to the forefront the essential nature of following Jesus as a way of life. Jesus said,

> Everyone then who hears these words of mine and does them will be like a wise man who built his house on the rock. And the rain fell, and the floods came, and the winds blew and beat on that house, but it did not fall, because it had been founded on the rock. And everyone who hears these words of mine and does not do them will be like a foolish man who built his house on the sand. And the rain fell, and the floods came, and the winds blew and beat against that house, and it fell, and great was the fall of it. (Matthew 7:24-27)

The difference between those whose house stood and those whose house fell was not in the hearing or not hearing but in doing or not doing. Many of us are aware of the words of Jesus, but what makes the difference is whether or not we are willing to implement what Jesus is teaching. Putting into practice the very words of Jesus becomes a solid foundation for us to build a good, stable, thriving life.

We have been drawn almost irresistibly to Jesus. I assume that is why most people desire to be disciples of Jesus. Each individual has their own story of coming to faith and beginning their Christian journey. Some people are raised in the faith and never have a conscious thought of life without the awareness of God. Other people come to faith later in life and have a dramatic story of conversion, from a life of death and destruction to a life of love and peace. I'm aware that many Christians carry the scars of broken relationships. People have let us down. People have betrayed us, wounded us, and told harsh stories built on fabricated lies . . . sadly, even members of the church have done this. The church has made plenty of mistakes—painful mistakes at times—but the church is still the gathering of people who follow Jesus. People may have let us down, but we have Jesus who is the healer of the pain inflicted by others. Jesus overwhelms us with his brightness and beauty. I'm constantly amazed by Jesus as he continues to be unfolded by the Spirit.

Jesus never changes. He is the way of the Lord, bestowing blessing on those who walk his way. He is our King and Lord, whose ways we walk in and find rootedness in life. Jesus is the way of love and life that never ends and the rock upon which we build our lives. When I became an intentional disciple of Jesus as a teenager, I began to live out my baptismal identity as a person identified by the death, burial, and resurrection of Jesus. Everything soon began to change after that prayer in my bedroom as a fifteen-year-old. On Sunday mornings I traded in my Cheerios and MTV for worship and Christian community. It took me a couple of months to grow comfortable with church, but once I responded to God's call to serve the church, I was all in. My friends and I would wear white shirts and ties to church. On one occasion our pastor said we looked like a bunch of Mormon missionaries. We weren't Mormon, but we did see ourselves as missionaries. I quickly sensed a call to vocational ministry and my high school became my mission field. What drew me to that church and that youth group, and indeed to the Christian faith, was Jesus! I was amazed and overwhelmed by Jesus. Years later I am still following Jesus because I am still amazed.

Before following Jesus I looked in the mirror and saw a breathing mass of insecurity. I suppose all teenagers struggle with self-worth and questions about identity, but my struggle seemed more pronounced. My family loved me. I knew this. But I felt a deep lingering disconnection in my heart. We had moved around a lot when I was a kid. As an introvert it was hard for me to make friends, and changing schools every couple of years didn't make it any easier. I tried to fit in and make friends when I moved into a new community, but constantly I was met with rejection. By high school I had a gnawing sense that I was simply unworthy of love. Then I came face to face with the God of love, the God fully embodied in Jesus. In the presence of Jesus I felt accepted without qualification. Rejection seemed to melt away. Jesus called me to follow him, and in the words of Robert Frost, he took me along the road less traveled by, "and that has made all the difference."

THE JESUS TRUTH PLUS THE JESUS WAY

Modern American evangelicals have made salvation something altogether different than discipleship. This was true of the kind of evangelicalism that nurtured my faith in my teens and twenties. Billy Graham–style evangelism and Campus Crusade's "Four Spiritual Laws" shaped the way I imagined evangelism. As I understood it, my role was to bear witness to Jesus in cooperation with the Holy Spirit who would convict people of the truth. Together we would work toward the goal of "getting people saved." Once they were "saved," we could make suggestions regarding next steps. With a fistful of yellow "Four Spiritual Laws" booklets, my goal was to plunder hell and populate heaven. But in my experience these varied forms of follow-up normally did not produce healthy flourishing disciples. Years later I would come to realize this method of evangelism wasn't what Jesus had called us to do.

Jesus didn't say, "Go into all the world and *get people saved*." He didn't say, "Get people to ask me into their hearts." He didn't say, "Go make good citizens of the empire." Jesus said, "Go therefore and make disciples of all nations" (Matthew 28:19). His words conveyed a clear command: Go into every person's world and invite people to become followers of Jesus. We are not called to manipulate people into making a decision. The way of Jesus is the way of invitation, not the way of manipulation. The constant call of Jesus wasn't "Ask me into your heart," but "Come follow me." The question we ask is not when did we "get saved," but when did we start participating in the life of salvation? Faithful followers of Jesus will make good citizens because Jesus teaches us to "render to Caesar the things that are Caesar's" (Matthew 22:21). However, making good citizens isn't the primary task of the church.

We come to Jesus in order to follow him because salvation is not found by asking Jesus into our lives, but by entering the life of Jesus where, as disciples, we find ourselves immersed in God's rescue plan. Much of the language in the New Testament is about our experience "in Christ." We enter into the life of Jesus more than Jesus enters our lives. If we go about asking Jesus into our hearts then it becomes easy for Jesus to become a character in the one-act play called "Me." A better way of talking about salvation is to talk about coming to Jesus and following him in order to walk in his ways by entering into his life. In this way, salvation and discipleship are much more intertwined.

The way of Jesus is the way to life, real life, real *human* life, the good life we have all innately longed for. Jesus said, "I am the way, and the truth, and the life. No one comes to the Father except through me" (John 14:6). We all want the life Jesus offers, even if we cannot completely articulate it. The life of Jesus is the water that will quench our deepest thirst and the bread that will satisfy our deepest desires. Jesus is the living water and the bread of life. Sadly, far too many people have assumed all that is necessary to experience that life is to confess the truth about Jesus. They have been told, "Pray this prayer. Say these words. Acknowledge this truth about Jesus. That's it. Do these things and you will experience eternal life." The problem is that people confess the Jesus truth and when they don't experience the Jesus life, they get frustrated and give up on the faith. What they are missing is the very thing Jesus called us to do. They are frustrated because they haven't yet learned to walk in Jesus' ways as disciples.

Confessing the truth about Jesus includes a kind of allegiance to Jesus. When we confess that we believe Jesus is Lord and Savior, we are trusting Jesus alone to lead us and to save us. Confessing the Jesus truth is what gets us into what Jesus is doing. Walking in the Jesus way keeps us in. We need both. As Eugene Peterson observed, "The Jesus way wedded to the Jesus truth brings about the Jesus life. We can't proclaim the Jesus truth but then do it any old way we like. Nor can we follow the Jesus way without speaking the Jesus truth."[4] Authentic disciples cannot cling to the truth about Jesus while avoiding the way of Jesus. The Jesus truth plus the Jesus way equals the Jesus life.

The Jesus truth is that he is God's Son and our Lord. Jesus is very God of very God, showing us what God is like. Jesus is equally our Lord, a rather archaic way of speaking of a person with authority. Our British neighbors across the Atlantic have a House of Lords and so perhaps the title "Lord" still carries meaning for them. For Americans the only time we use the world *lord* is when we are talking about a landlord. Those of us who have rented a house or apartment understand what a landlord is. My wife and I rented for the first five years we were married, two houses and one apartment. When we were in the last house we rented, Jenni wanted to hang a wallpaper border in the kitchen. As much as we wanted to add some color in the kitchen, we couldn't without the permission of the landlord. If we wanted to paint the walls, we couldn't apply one drop of paint without permission because the walls of that house did not belong to us. They belonged to the landlord. When we confess the truth that Jesus is Lord, we are confessing that our lives no longer belong to us. They belong to Jesus. We just live here. Jesus now owns the right to our lives.

Confessing the Jesus truth is not enough to experience the Jesus life. We must also walk in the Jesus way. Paul's words

are clear: "Therefore, as you received Christ Jesus the Lord,
so walk in him, rooted and built up in him and established in
the faith" (Colossians 2:6-7). Jesus is the way to be truly and
fully human, because Jesus is fully human. We were created
by God as human beings to bear God's image, to reflect God's
image into creation, and to reflect creation's praise back to
God. Sin twists us out of shape, so that we reflect a broken
image. The way of Jesus is the way to be fully alive and thus
fully human. The way of Jesus has been laid out for us in the
Sermon on the Mount. It is the way of forgiveness, peace, and
reconciling love. It is the radical way of truth, faithfulness,
and enemy-love; the way of prayer, faith, and self-giving love.
Not only do we experience the Jesus life when we walk in
the Jesus way; we also become the means by which God is
rescuing the world.

If we are going to make disciples, then we must start by
becoming disciples ourselves. So ask yourself, "Do I want to
follow Jesus?" In the end we all do what we want to do. So do
you want to follow Jesus? Maybe you are struggling with that
desire. Maybe you know intellectually that you ought to follow Jesus, but your desires are headed in a different direction.
That's okay. You can ask for God the Holy Spirit to change
your desires, so that your *ought to* becomes your *want to*. So
what do you want to do? When blind Bartimaeus stood before
Jesus his need was clear, but Jesus still asked, "What do you
want me to do for you?" In this moment, Jesus is asking you,
"What do you want? Do you want to follow me, confessing
my truth, walking in my ways, and experiencing my life?" If
your answer is yes, then join us in this adventure of becoming
a disciple of Jesus.

discussion **questions**

1. Did you ever play follow-the-leader when you were a kid? Did you like it? What was your favorite childhood game?

2. What were the circumstances around your coming to Jesus and choosing to follow him? How did you feel? Was the process quick or gradual? Or did it have twists and setbacks?

3. What do you find most attractive about Jesus? What draws you to follow him?

4. If following Jesus is being an apprentice who does while the master watches, what is Jesus watching you do these days?

5. Who are the weakest, most vulnerable people in your world? How should followers of Jesus care for them?

6. How has your experience with the love of God brought change in your life?

7. What does the life Jesus offers look like? How does walking in the Jesus way help you experience that life?

8. Imagine Jesus as the landlord of your life. How does that change what you do and don't do?

9. What do you want Jesus to do for you? What are you willing to do for him?

10. What steps do you need to take this week to walk in the ways of Jesus?

2

Story

The Way of the Gospel

We are a storytelling people. Some are more skilled in the artistry of storytelling than others, but we all have a story. You could say we are the stories we tell. As a pastor I don't work with numbers and dollars or brick and mortar. I don't work with heavy machinery or computer codes. I work with people. I have spent countless hours sitting in coffee shops and restaurants, homes and hospitals, engaged in conversation with people. In my work as a pastor, I am particularly interested in connecting with new people, those who are new to the faith or new to our church. I like making those initial introductions to people who feel on the outside, on the margins. Maybe it's my Southern heritage, but I always want to invite people into what Jesus is doing in and through the church. I don't want people to feel lost or excluded.

Discipleship begins with hospitality after all. If we are going to obey Jesus' command to make disciples, then we need the practices of hospitality that welcome people into the kingdom of God. Hospitality lays claim to those very simple practices of opening doors, sharing a meal, and striking up a conversation.

When I meet someone for the first time at a coffee shop, after we pick our seats, exchange pleasantries, and take our first sips of coffee, I typically make the same request: "So, tell me your story." Inexplicably people respond with a confused look and vocalized pause. We haven't been conditioned to get to know people according to their story. We typically want to gather facts about a person by either stalking them on social media or asking fact-finding questions. "What do you do? Tell me about your family. Do you like dogs? Do you like cats? What do you do for fun?" I'm all in favor of these kinds of questions. It's helpful for me to know if I am talking to a dog person or a cat person. While these questions allow me to know certain things about a person, they don't help me get to know that individual. I need to know their story and they need to know mine. A person I'm meeting for the first time can easily learn facts about me. I can ramble on about my vocation, my height, my family, my pets, and my idiosyncrasies, but I am not the sum total of these facts. I am the stories I tell.

I typically respond to the vocalized pause and awkward silence that follows with a smile and encouragement. I'll say something like, "Everyone has a story to tell. It is the story of your life. You may not think it is that exciting, but telling our stories is how we get to know each other." These words of encouragement normally set their minds at ease and people then follow up with the question, "Where should I start?" To which I always respond, "At the beginning." This brief instruction yields incredible results. Most people start talking. Those who have had their trust receptors damaged unfold their story cautiously, offering brief details. Most people jump right into their stories, loaded with subtle and vivid detail, and I settle back in my seat, hold my coffee in my hands, and listen. These stories often capture their moments of struggle and triumph, the important events that have shaped them, and the people they have become. Telling our stories can be messy and disjointed; sometimes I must break into their storytelling to ask for dates so I can follow the chronology of their history. As I listen and follow their journeys in my imagination, I'm amazed at how ordinary people have lived such fascinating lives.

God is the master storyteller and God is writing the very detailed story of each of us as followers of Jesus. Learning to tell our stories takes time and a lot of editing, particularly as we grow as disciples and become more attuned to the story God is writing in us. The way I tell my story today is slightly different from the way I told it ten years ago. The editing never stops because God never reaches the end of the work of grace in us. We never have to let hope completely drain out of our hearts, because the master storyteller never quits on us. No matter how bad things get, God is with us. He has his pen to the paper of our hearts, crossing through errant lines and ill-fitting paragraphs. God doesn't waste any words—he just has a way of rearranging them in a way that creates something beautiful.

God writes our individual stories, but if we take a step back from ourselves for a moment, we can see something else. God has authored a big, all-encompassing story that affects all of us. This story transcends nations, cultures, languages, and people spread throughout history. It's a story of God's love for the world, a love story for all of us. A story we call the gospel.

THE GOOD NEWS

The gospel is the central message of the Christian faith. It is quite literally good news. The very word *evangelical* comes from the Greek word *euangelion* ("good news"). Within evangelicalism it's common to hear things like:

"We need to go preach the gospel."

"Go share the gospel."

"We are gospel-centered."

I add an enthusiastic Amen to each of these statements. In following Jesus we walk in the way of the gospel. We should most certainly be about the work of preaching and sharing the gospel. I wonder though if we know what we mean when we use the word *gospel*. In the words of Inigo Montoya from the 1989 movie *The Princess Bride*, "You keep using that word. I do not think it means what you think it means." We, myself included, have the tendency to misunderstand the gospel, and for good reason. The gospel is a Jewish story first told in a Roman world communicated to us in the Greek language which most of us read in an English translation. Understanding the essence of the gospel affects the contours of the lives we live as followers of Jesus. If we misunderstand the gospel we hear when we come to Jesus, then we will misjudge the steps we take in following after Jesus.

Before we look at the nature of the gospel, let's review what the gospel is not.

The gospel isn't a collections of how-tos. In this regard the gospel isn't simply good advice or a set of moral instructions. Modern evangelicalism is the product of the Enlightenment filtered through the American experiment . . . and we always-industrious Americans love to learn how to do new things. Today, evangelicals tend to drift toward a practical how-to approach to the faith. Following Jesus is fundamentally a practice, but the gospel which gives birth to disciples is not itself a pragmatic tool to be used. As an expression of this kind of pragmatism, evangelicals at a popular level tend to misinterpret the gospel in terms of what we do, but the gospel isn't a how-to. It isn't

- how to get saved
- how to go to heaven after we die
- how to have a personal relationship with God
- how to experience forgiveness
- how to be a better person

Certainly each of the how-tos represents an important aspect of following Jesus. We experience God's salvation as followers of Jesus. We need a thoroughly biblical understanding of heaven and a renewed hope in the God of heaven. We cannot rely on another's knowledge of God; we need to know God for ourselves. In loving God, we order our lives in such a way that we prioritize our relationship with God. Forgiveness remains at the heart of our work of reconciliation where we turn hate into love, bitterness into hope, and sorrow into dancing. By God's grace we all become better as we become more like Jesus. All of these aspects of discipleship are important, but none of them are themselves the gospel.

The gospel is also not a collection of God-facts. Evangelicalism has its historical roots in the Protestant Reformation of the sixteenth century. The Reformers sought to critique the practices of the Roman Catholic Church by making an appeal to the Bible over church tradition. The lasting good that came from their protest was an elevated view of Scripture. Throughout the history of the church, the preaching of the gospel has suffered whenever followers of Jesus devalued the sacredness of Scripture. But the gospel is not a set of theological opinions propped up by our collection of Bible verses. The gospel isn't bits of information we know about God or how God saves us. The cross remains at the center of our faith, but the gospel is not a certain theory of atonement. We are saved by Jesus and through Jesus' sacrificial death and subsequent resurrection, but our sophisticated and preferred understanding of how exactly Jesus' death saves us is not the same thing as the gospel. (We will explore the death of Jesus and what it means to walk in the way of the cross in more detail in the next chapter.) The gospel includes Jesus' death, but the gospel is neither shorthand for the summation of all Christian doctrine nor the summation of one doctrine like "justification by faith." The gospel is neither the benefits of one's faith nor the practice of living out one's faith. The gospel gives shape to these, but they are not the gospel themselves.

The gospel is a story. It is the very true story of Jesus: the story of how the kingdom of God came from heaven to earth through Jesus' life, death, resurrection, and ascension. In the first-century world of Jesus and the apostles, people heard the word *gospel* as an imperial message, good news coming from Rome. A gospel announcement was like an official press release from the Roman emperor. Contained in that message would have been a royal announcement that something had happened. This news implied that something else would happen in the future as a result of this event. Things were about to change. It wasn't clear whether this change was for the better or for the worse, but one thing was certain—life in the present was different. According to N. T. Wright, this past-future-present understanding of gospel is what early Christians meant when they talked about the good news of King Jesus. "Something *had happened* because of which everything was now different. Something *would happen* that would complete this initial victory. . . . As a result, *the present moment was new and different*."[1] As a story, the gospel is the announcement that in and through Jesus: (1) something has happened, (2) something will happen, and (3) everything is now new and different.

THE BIG NEWS

Have you ever had big news that was so earth-shattering that you felt like you were about to burst? News so life changing that you needed to catch your breath and funnel all your excitement into a creative way to announce it to the world? Some young couples attempt to share this kind of news through increasingly popular gender-reveal parties. After a couple announces their pregnancy and learns the sex of the baby, they gather friends and family together to reveal the gender by cutting a cake which is either pink or blue on the inside.

My wife and I decided to develop a creative plan to tell my parents that we were pregnant with our first child, their first grandchild. More than anything we wanted to surprise my father, who had been bugging us about grandchildren for years. My wife and I had been married for over three years and I was in the last year of seminary when we found out she was pregnant. I remember the joy and tears we shared when she took the pregnancy test and it turned out to be positive. Our little two-bedroom apartment seemed to glow and vibrate with excitement that day.

My parents had planned to come visit us for Thanksgiving that year and we thought that visit would be the perfect time to tell them our good news. We told them we wanted to exchange

Christmas gifts with them on this particular visit, since we wouldn't see them at Christmastime that year. We had a ball cap embroidered for my dad that said, "I'm going to be a Paw Paw." I called my grandfather "Paw Paw," and my dad had made it clear that he wanted to be called by the same name. We swathed the hat in white tissue paper, stuffed it in a nondescript cardboard box, wrapped it up and waited for them to arrive.

Waiting when anticipation is boiling just under the surface is no fun. When they arrived, we played it cool. Hugs were shared. Pleasantries were exchanged. We sat down for an uneventful meal and then the time came to exchange gifts in the living room.

"Dad, why don't you wait and open your gift last," I said, trying to muffle my excitement.

When his turn came to open his gift, I watched his eyes, preparing myself to gauge his response to the message on the hat once he read it. He tore through the wrapping paper and used a pocket knife to break the tape holding the lid of the cardboard box together. He pulled out the tissue paper in no particular hurry. As he held the hat, I watched his eyes reading the message. He looked up at me with squinted eyes of bewilderment. Not the reaction I was expecting.

"Ha. Ha. Very funny. I know I will be a Paw Paw *someday*," he said.

"Some day?" I thought to myself.

"*No* dad." I countered. "You are going to be a Paw Paw soon. We're pregnant!!!"

A blank look of disbelief flashed across his face.

"No . . . no . . . no," was all my mom could say.

Though I played this scenario through in my head dozens and dozens of times before this moment, I never anticipated a reaction of disbelief. I expected lots of excitement or maybe some questions like *How are you going to have a baby while in seminary? How are you going to afford this? Are you buying a house? What about moving after seminary?* In my planning and in all of the mounting anticipation, I never expected the shock I saw on their faces.

"No, really. We are pregnant. Seriously," I said with all sincerity, and yet their blank stares remained. Then I had an idea. I walked down the hall into the bedroom where Jenni had a pile of pregnancy and parenting books on her nightstand. I grabbed a stack of four or five of these books and walked back into the living room. I slammed them down on the coffee table and declared in my best preacher voice, "WE ARE HAVING A BABY!!!" The impact of the books hitting the hard wood of the coffee table made an impact on their brains. Blank stares turned into bright smiles. We all stood and hugged. This announcement was big news!

Something had happened to Jenni and me. We were pregnant. Something was going to happen. We were going to have a baby and none of the books we read had us prepared for how things were going to change. But because of this news, everything had become new and different. My son had not even been born yet, but I felt different. My thinking was different. I still had a lot of growing up to do, but I was no longer the same.

LORD JESUS IS KING JESUS

The gospel is the big news that Jesus is Lord. Bruxy Cavey calls this short statement "the gospel in three words," a simple but life-changing phrase. We do not confess "Jesus is Lord" in order to acquire something from Jesus and then move on with our lives. According to Cavey, "Jesus is not just a means to an end, a ticket to get into heaven, or a way to 'get saved.' Rather, Jesus is our Leader, our Lover, our Lord here and now. And that is life changing while we live, not just life prolonging when we die."[2] The gospel message that Jesus is Lord is the big news that something has happened, something *will* happen, and now everything is new and different. To confess Jesus is Lord implies that the one confessing has submitted to Jesus' leadership.

Unfortunately much of the talk about Jesus as Lord reduces Jesus to a religious category, where we assume Jesus is Lord of our "beliefs," or our religious lives, but certainly not our real lives. Everything becomes new and different when we declare Jesus is Lord, because in doing so we are giving up the rights we have to our lives. We are saying that our lives no longer belong to us; now they belong to Jesus, our landlord. Another word for "lord" is *king*, still an archaic word, but one that captures our imagination. Lord Jesus is King Jesus. This is the gospel. God's kingdom has come through King Jesus. "Christ" is not Jesus' last name, but a title meaning "king," specifically the Jewish king. The Hebrew word for "king" is *anointed one* or *messiah*, because Jewish people did not coronate their kings—they anointed them with oil. Jesus came in fulfillment of all of Israel's prophets to be Israel's king. The God of Israel had always desired to be king of his people. God accommodated himself to the wishes of his people by giving Israel a king even though up to that point *he* had been their king (1 Samuel 12:12-13). The psalmists declared with all boldness that God was not only king over Israel, but over all nations. Imagine that daring claim. Israel was just one small, seemingly insignificant people group. Countless other tribes, ethnic groups, and nations surrounded them, each worshiping the deity over their geographic region of the earth, and yet the children of Abraham had the audacity to proclaim that their God was the king of all other gods and earthly kings. In King Jesus, the God of Israel came to rule and reign not just over one strip of land adjacent to the Mediterranean Sea. King Jesus rules over all nations as Israel's Messiah and the world's true Lord. This is big news. This is the gospel.

THE BIBLE IN FIVE PARTS

We cannot make sense of this news unless we hear it in the context of the big story the Bible is telling. The gospel as the story of Jesus becoming Lord and King is the climax of the story of Scripture itself. The Bible is a collection of lots of different kinds of writings inspired by the Holy Spirit, collected by the church, and given to us that we might hear the gospel and see Jesus. Through the Old Testament and New Testament we find a fascinating collection of history, wisdom literature, songs, poetry, prophecy, biography, letters, and apocalyptic end-of-the-world literature. The various writers were moved by the Holy Spirit as they wrote books, letters, prayers, and poetry. Holy Scripture is the table where Christians for centuries have come to sit to be nourished in the ways of Jesus. Through Bible translation, the proliferation of book publishing, and modern technology, the Scriptures have never been more accessible, but we do not treat them as common. For followers of Jesus the Bible is a sacred text finding no equal among anything else ever written in human history.

We hold the Bible in high regard not only for its inspiration and sacredness but also for its cultural complexity. For example, if we want to know what Jesus himself taught, we have to work through at least four layers of language. If English is your first language, then you read what has been translated into English from a Greek text written by one of the gospel writers. But Jesus did not speak Greek. He spoke Aramaic . . . but he came from a Hebrew culture where he learned prayers and scripture in Hebrew. He spoke from a Hebrew mindset. So to understand Jesus, we read in English what has been translated from Greek based on what was spoken in Aramaic from a Hebrew mind! We need the help of a community, including the community of biblical scholars, as well as the Holy Spirit if we are going to read Scripture responsibly.

With full acknowledgment of the diversity and complexity of Scripture, we do find a cohesive story arc with a definite beginning, middle, and end. A helpful way to see the big story the Bible tells is to break up the story into five parts:

- Part 1: Creation
- Part 2: Corruption
- Part 3: Covenant
- Part 4: Christ
- Part 5: New creation

The Bible opens with *creation*. In the beginning God created everything—light and dark, land and sea, plants and animals, and then humanity, male and female. Everything was good. The days of creation were days of forming and filling. God formed the skies and filled them with the sun, moon, and stars. God formed the seas and filled them with marine life. God formed the land and filled it with trees, grass, and creeping things. Everything God made was good. The soil of the fields and the souls of the humans were all good. Creation reverberated with the goodness of God as God fashioned a dwelling place, a place where God could kick off his shoes and put up his feet. The earth was created to be God's footstool (Isaiah 66:1).

Then things went terribly wrong. Early in the story, *corruption* slithered into God's good creation. God gave Adam and Eve a garden and instructed them to eat from any tree including the tree of life, but not from the tree of the knowledge of good and evil. God wanted to be their source of knowledge. God didn't want humanity stumbling about trying to do life on their own. The snake entered into the garden, planting seeds of doubt: "Did God *really* say . . . ?" Their doubt quickly grew into cynicism and then disobedience. They failed and were kicked out of the garden, exiled to a foreign land. Corruption continued to spread like a virus. Brother betrayed brother. Cain killed Abel. Evil and violence begin to overtake what was supposed to be a peaceful garden. The escalation of evil ended with destruction and a flood. From the ark, Noah released a dove that didn't rest until it descended on the shoulder of the Prince of Peace. Corruption continued to spread until humanity tried to reach God through the construction of a tower.

God chose *covenant* as the answer to the exponential problems created by corruption. God promised to make out of Abraham a great nation. In this promise, God said Abraham and his descendants would be blessed, and through Abraham, God would bless all the families of the earth. The people of Abraham grew into the nation of Israel, the chosen people. They were chosen not so God could damn the rest of the nations to eternal destruction, but in order to set right a corrupt and broken down world. God gave them law in order to form them into a community of worship and justice, but, sadly, corruption took hold of Israel too. Idolatry and the subsequent injustice and immorality persisted among them, resulting in a divided kingdom and ultimately exile. Within this covenant, God sent prophets who spoke of the promise of a king, a son of Abraham, the true son of David, a prophet like Moses. In the reign of this king the mountains would be brought low and the valleys pushed high. Swords would be turned into plows. Destruction would no longer be found. The story of God's covenant with Israel comes to an end without a conclusion. The shackles of exile keep Israel bound as prisoners in their own land and the covenant people of God are left waiting.

Then something happens! *Christ* Jesus steps onto the world's stage as the long-awaited conclusion to the story of Israel. He came through the womb of the virgin Mary who had become pregnant by the Holy Spirit. Jesus came as Israel's Messiah and the world's true Lord. Jesus proclaimed God's kingdom. He taught and healed the people. Jesus formed a new community out of those who answered his call to follow him. He challenged the religious establishment and offered forgiveness to sinners. Then the earthly powers colluded and sentenced Jesus to death. He died on a Roman cross. He was buried and descended to the dwelling of the dead. Then Jesus conquered death itself though his resurrection. He appeared to his followers and then ascended to the right hand of God. Through the birth, life, death, resurrection, and ascension of Jesus something most certainly had happened. Plus, something *will* happen: restoration and justice for all. And now everything is new and different for those who follow Jesus.

God's good creation will not be subject to corruption forever. God's covenant plan that started with Abraham and was fulfilled in Christ will reach its desired objective—*new creation*. Like a master craftsman restoring a historic home,

God will make everything new. God has no plans to bring in a cosmic wrecking ball to demolish his good world and rebuild from the ground up; God will restore the natural beauty of this beaten up world. Eventually God will even bring together heaven and earth, so that God will dwell with his people forever. Evil will be cast out once and for all and God will make all things right.

I'VE BEEN SAVED

The climax of the story told by the Bible is the gospel, the Jesus story, the big news. Jesus is the something that has happened. Everything will be made right in the future and now, in the present, there exists the real potential for everything to become different and new. Jesus has died for our sins. God has raised Jesus from the dead for our salvation. The word *salvation* is overladen with so many religious clichés that many of us have lost sight that at its core salvation implies rescue. When God saves us, God rescues us from death, destruction, sin, and hell in order to bring us safely to the good life—eternal life. You are invited to believe this good news, trust in this royal announcement, and experience salvation at the intersection of the Jesus story and your story.

When we hear the gospel and turn to Jesus in faith and repentance, we are able to echo Paul's words, "For I am not ashamed of the gospel, for it is the power of God for salvation to everyone who believes, to the Jew first and also to the Greek" (Romans 1:16). Salvation is more than a status. It's more of a transformational partnership than a transactional event. It's helpful to see sin as more a sickness from which humanity needs healing than a crime that requires a legal pardon. We will explore this idea in more detail in the next chapter. If we see our problem as primarily a legal one where we broke God's rules and need to be punished, then salvation becomes the means by which we are acquitted. That is true, but our Scriptures reveal that there is more to the story. If we see our problem as primarily a therapeutic one, we see that sin destroys our human identity as God's image bearers in the world. From this perspective salvation becomes the means by which we are healed, transformed, and changed. If we only view sin through the lens of the courtroom, we miss both the destructive systems of sin and the corrupting properties of sin.

The problem with sin is not merely that we have broken the rules and deserve to be punished. Sin has broken us and we need to be mended. Both the imagery of the courtroom and the imagery of healing are true. Both metaphors are used in the New Testament, but the therapeutic version shows us that salvation is more *transformational* than *transactional*. A transactional view is a one-time event, whereas the transformational view is a lifelong process. Within the transactional view, the primary mission of the church mutates into plans to go and get people to make a decision, to decide in their hearts what they think about Jesus. After they "get saved" we try to sell them on some kind of optional discipleship program. But Jesus did not tell us to go into all the world and "get people to make up in their minds what they believe about me." Jesus told us to go into all the world and make disciples, wherein we find God's salvation.

Through this rescuing work God rewrites our stories, but only if we come in contact with the gospel story, which is the story of Jesus. Our first step is to accept Jesus' invitation to become a disciple. In this regard, experiencing salvation and becoming a disciple go hand in hand. We do not follow Jesus to impress God with our moral performance. The plot of the gospel isn't what we do for God, but what God has done for us. The gospel is how God has become king of the world through Jesus. In following Jesus we turn to him and say yes to his rule and reign. The way of the gospel is one of partnering with God, who loves. We no longer need to think that we must keep the rules in order to somehow convince God to love us. That way is the way of legalistic, rule-keeping religion. The way of the gospel is the way of true and undefiled religion with Jesus at the center. God is with us every step of the way through the Holy Spirit. We grow in this way when we accept the fact that we are loved by God and nothing will ever change that fact. God loves us. God is for us. God is with us. The gospel story becomes our new identity.

We all need a story big enough to help us make sense of the world. It's common for our minds to make up a story whenever we lack information. The gospel gives us the very true story of Jesus, a story bigger than us, a story of God's never-ending love. Once we lose ourselves in this story, we discover who we are supposed to be. As we enter into the gospel story we become people of the cross and resurrection: people of the Spirit. This gospel shapes the contours of our mission. We are gathered by the gospel that we may be scattered into the world.

discussion **questions**

1. Describe a time when you were really sick. What was that experience like?

2. When you think about your own story, what are some important details in the beginning, middle, and end?

3. How do you feel knowing that God is continually writing and rewriting your story?

4. What is one of the "big news" events in your life? How did you feel in sharing this news with others?

5. If Jesus is King as the gospel proclaims then how should we live as citizens of God's kingdom? What is the proper way to respond to Jesus as King?

6. In what ways does the Bible provide answers for you? In what ways does it provoke questions?

7. How do you see the Bible leading you to Jesus?

8. What does it mean for you to experience salvation at the intersection of the Jesus story and your story?

9. What are the key differences between seeing sin as rule breaking and sin as a sickness?

10. How do you need to rework the telling of your own story in light of the Jesus story?

3

Cruciform

The Way of the Cross

When I was in high school I wanted to be an athlete, but my athletic ability tended to fall way behind my desire. I wanted to be a great basketball player, but as much as I loved playing pickup games in driveways and gyms throughout my hometown, I wasn't very good. Before the surge of my faith in Jesus during my sophomore year of high school, my bedroom had become somewhat of a shrine to Michael Jordan. After my turn to Jesus, I tore the posters down like King Josiah in the Old Testament tearing down altars to false gods. But before Jesus, my devotion was directed to Jordan. "Like Mike. If I can be like Mike" was my mantra. In my mind, when I set foot on the basketball court I was Michael Jordan playing for the Bulls. In reality, I looked more like Michael Scott from *The Office*. At times I would daydream about becoming a professional basketball player. Isn't this the dream of all kids at some time during childhood and early adolescence? Don't all kids dream of being a professional athlete or musician at some point during their life?

I also ran track during high school and I soon found out that I was a better sprinter running 110-meter high hurdles than I was as a power forward in basketball. I loved the thrill of competition. I still do. I loved the speed and fluidity of hurdling. As I learned from my coach, you do not *jump* over the hurdles; rather, the act of hurdling becomes an extension of your stride. I loved pushing myself physically. I loved seeing results and I loved winning. After becoming an intentional follower of Jesus, I wanted to honor Jesus with all of my life, including sports. As I warmed up for a race at every track meet, I would wear a T-shirt over my jersey as a canvas for the cross around my neck. The cross was made out of woven skinny black-and-white nylon rope; I had picked it up at a DC Talk concert in the early 1990s. The band DC Talk was a bunch of Jesus freaks and so was I. As I would go through warm-up exercises on the track I could feel that lightweight cross slapping against my chest. It had become for me a reminder of both Jesus' love for the world and my newfound identity in Jesus.

THE REVOLUTIONARY CROSS

Crosses have become a fixture in American culture as a fashionable accessory. Everyone from celebrities to custodians wears a cross around their neck. It's no longer the exclusive emblem of followers of Jesus. The cross has transcended the status of mere religious symbol. Yet for those of us who believe in King Jesus, the cross is revolutionary. The crucifixion of Jesus marked the beginning of a new day, a rebellion against the ways of empire, the ways of power, idolatry, and corruption. At the cross, Jesus became King. His death announced a new ruling authority on the earth: King Jesus. We have entered his kingdom, the kingdom of King Jesus, and for us the message of the cross is nothing less than the power of God (1 Corinthians 1:18).

The cross in Jesus' day was neither a religious symbol nor a fashion piece. The cross was the implement of torture and death used by the Romans to execute violent criminals and political rebels. Jesus grew up in a Jewish family in an occupied nation. Israel was under the boot of Rome, an empire that ruled with a ruthless authority. Growing up in Galilee in the early part of the first century, Jesus would have experienced Jewish revolts and he would have seen with his own eyes how Jewish rebels were handled. Would-be Jewish kings rose to prominence while Jesus was a child. These leaders would amass a following and charge after Rome with the sword. The result was always the same. Rome would crush the rebellion and crucify those who tried to challenge it. It is easy to imagine that while traveling with his father to some carpentry job, a young Jesus would have looked up to see Jewish revolutionaries dying on Roman crosses of wood. Jesus grew up in the shadow of the cross.

The Romans were not the first to practice execution by crucifixion, but they certainly perfected it into a hideous and terrifying form of punishment. Those who were crucified were stripped naked and nailed to the wood, their bodies twisted grotesquely. They would suffer for hours or even days. The goal was not just to execute criminals but to humiliate them. Rome publicly crucified political dissidents, traitors, rebels, leaving their rotting corpses on crosses to serve as a stern warning to the masses—DON'T. MESS. WITH. ROME.

Make no mistake, Jesus died as a political rebel, a rival king. Rome did not execute Jesus because he was trying to start a new religion. Jesus was arrested and crucified as the powers of religion and empire colluded together to take out a political threat. The sign attached to Jesus' cross read "Jesus of Nazareth, the King of the Jews" (John 19:19). Jesus died as a king. His crown was thorns. His throne was a cross. The principalities and powers intended that his crucifixion be his greatest moment of humiliation, but it was the moment of his exaltation. In Jesus' crucifixion and through Jesus' resurrection, God indeed made him "both Lord and Christ" (Acts 2:36). We don't make Jesus Lord by asking him to be our "personal" Lord and Savior. God made Jesus Lord by raising him from the dead. If we are following Jesus we are having personal encounters with the resurrected and ascended Jesus. We exercise personal faith in him daily. But he is not our personal or private Lord; he is the Messiah, the Son of the living God ruling the nations.

The Jewish people of Jesus' day were waiting for the Messiah to come and "restore the kingdom of Israel" (Acts 1:6). They were not waiting for the Messiah to forgive them of their sins and take individual souls to heaven when they die. Their longing was for the Messiah to come, forgive them of their sins, and redeem Israel (Luke 24:21). God chose Israel so that through Israel he could bless all the families of the earth. God chose Israel to be his own people not merely to have a preferred relationship with one nation, but so that this nation of royal priests would be a light of worship and justice to all the nations of the world. In Jesus, the God of Israel was becoming King of the nations. The Jewish prophets promised that the Messiah would come to be that King and inherit all the nations of the world. When Paul wrote, "For I delivered to you as of first importance what I also received: that Christ died for our sins *in accordance with the Scriptures*" (1 Corinthians 15:3), he did not mean that Jesus died according to a couple of select verses in the Old Testament. "In accordance with the Scriptures" refers to all of the Jewish Scriptures which tell us the complex up-and-down story of Israel. In other words, the very true story of Jesus' death is the very surprising ending to the story of Israel. It just wasn't the ending Israel was looking for or anticipating.

Israel's prophets spoke of a coming King, the Messiah who would bring the rule of heaven to earth. Jewish followers of Jesus understood his death as a failure. When Jesus died, all of their messianic dreams died, because a crucified messiah is a failed messiah. "Cursed is everyone who is hanged on a tree" (Galatians 3:13). Jesus took on the curse of the law so the blessing of Abraham might expand to incorporate both Jews and Gentiles. Jesus died for our redemption, as the atoning sacrifice for our sin. He died as both our Savior and our King. The cross is the symbol of the arrival of God's kingdom from heaven to earth and also the way the kingdom comes. The kingdom of God doesn't come through amassing power and chest-thumping might, but through humility and suffering. The death of King Jesus signaled the beginning of a kingdom revolution, the rule of God conquering sin and all the darkness connected to it: all of our guilt, shame, idolatry, injustice, immorality, and even death itself.

SWALLOWING UP SIN

When we confess Jesus as Lord and believe wholeheartedly that God raised him from the dead, we open our hearts to the possibility of cleansing, healing, liberation, and transformation from sin. In a letter, John Wesley once described sin as "voluntary transgression." Wesley wrote, "Nothing is sin particularly speaking, but a voluntary transgression of the known law of God. Therefore, every voluntary breach of the law of love is sin; and nothing else, if we speak properly."[1] This proper definition of sin was fitting for those outside the Christian faith.

Wesley had a slightly different understanding of sin for those living in Christ. When referring to sin and Christians, Wesley pointed to sins of the heart as, "any disposition contrary to the mind which was in Christ."[2] Wesley had the foresight to see and describe sin as both corrupt behaviors and a corrupt heart. However, the holiness and evangelical traditions of the eighteenth and nineteenth centuries which followed him tended to emphasize sin in terms of behavior. For Holiness Christians, sin was doing wrong things, breaking one of the many rules from drinking alcohol to dancing in public (or dancing in private for that matter). Evangelical Christians understand God sent Jesus to save us from our sins, to give us a new heart, so we won't do sinful things anymore. While the corruption of the human heart finds some space in a popular evangelical understanding of sin, behavior remains the focus of all talk of sin. A more holistic way of looking at sin beyond mere voluntary transgression or willful disobedience is to imagine sin as our drawing back from the way of love. According to Thomas Merton, "All sin is rooted in the failure of love. All sin is a withdrawal of love from God, in order to love something else."[3] Our tendency to pull away from love is a sickness affecting us all.

I lived for forty years without ever having the flu. I had this unbelievably great track record of not getting sick until the flu snuck up on me a couple of years ago and knocked me out. My wife and I had spent a Saturday afternoon in the winter installing a new backsplash in the kitchen at my mother-in-law's house. As we were finishing up, a creeping achiness began to sneak up my back and I slowly sank down to the kitchen floor, leaning my back against the hard cabinet. I assumed I was just tired. Nope. The flu was just beginning to settle in. My wife and I headed home and within two hours we were both wrapped up in blankets, shivering, coughing, and feverish. It's hard enough when one of us is sick, but this scenario was worse; we were both sick with the flu, at the exact same time.

For the next couple of days I wandered around the house like a nomad. Wrapped up in an old quilt, covering up my sickness-attire of sweat pants, wool socks, hoodie, and faded Kansas City Chiefs hat, I would meander to the kitchen to get a drink, trying to keep the fluids going. Then I would slowly find my way back to the couch in the living room where my feverish body, lethargic and lifeless, found a temporary home. We attended to the kids the best we could, but for a couple days we lay around zombie-like, energy-less shells of our former selves. We returned to health after a few days and within a week or so our energy levels returned and we felt like ourselves again. At one point while I sat in my quilted cocoon, praying for my fever to break, I had a thought: the flu is to our bodies what sin is to our souls.

The flu, as with all sickness and disease, belongs to the dark world of death. Jesus has come to give us a flourishing human life. Jesus died for our sins, not because God has a giant score-card next to his throne where he has marked down every sinful thing we have done. Certainly this metaphor has its place, as we have seen in Wesley's understanding of sin, but it may not be the most helpful. Jesus died for our sins because sin is a sickness affecting the human soul. Sin has corrupted all of God's good creation and we are not immune; it has infected all of us. Sin slithered its way into our story in Genesis 3 and displayed its feverish corruption in humanity's disobedience and subsequent shame and blame. This sickness was documented in Cain killing Abel in Genesis 4 and demonstrated with the increased corruption and violence in Genesis 6. Finally it culminated in humanity's misguided attempt to make a name for themselves without God in Genesis 11. The fall of humanity, described vividly in Genesis 3–11, was not so much a fall from God's good graces as it was a fall from God's good design for humanity.

The sickness of sin has infected us all. This sickness has twisted and perverted us, so that outside of Christ, we are subhuman. When we hurt one another, when we mistreat one another, or commit acts of exploitation, injustice, or idolatry, we are not being "just human." All too often after people make a mistake, they excuse their misdeed by saying, "I'm only human." This admission is often uttered with sincerity, but it isn't true. When we act out of our sickness and lie, harm, steal, or exploit we are not "being human." We are being less than human. We have all grown up in and among subhumans and have wrongly assumed that moral failure at any level is an integral human trait. It isn't. To live out of our human sickness of sin is to be dead (Ephesians 2:1-5). Not that we are literally incapable of doing anything morally acceptable, but we are hampered by death much like when my wife and I were sick with the flu. I was able to move about the house and do a few things when I was sick, but not much!

To be truly human requires a healer; we must be healed from the human sickness of sin. Jesus is that healer. Jesus heals us from sin by taking our sin away. When John the Baptist saw Jesus approaching him, John proclaimed, "Behold, the Lamb of God, who takes away the sin of the world" (John 1:29). King Jesus became an atoning sacrifice for sin on the cross by becoming the place where all the sin of the world was brought together at a single point in history and condemned by God in the Son of God's skin. King Jesus died with our sin, swallowing it up. He became the Lamb of God who takes away the sin of the world, so we could be freed from sin, free to become our true selves. Those who believe in him, who have crossed through the waters of baptism, can now say, "There is therefore now no condemnation for those who are in Christ Jesus" (Romans 8:1). King Jesus takes away our sin, but first he takes it on himself. Think back to the suffering of Jesus, beginning with his arrest:

Judas betrayed Jesus with a kiss.

His friends deserted him.

Herod's guards slapped him.

Soldiers mocked him with a crown of thorns.

Pilate's guards punched him.

Pilate had him scourged, the flesh on the back of the Son of God unmercifully ripped open.

He was forced to carry his cross uphill and when he came to a place that was called "the Skull," he was crucified. He stretched out his loving arms upon the hard wood of the cross and soldiers drove nails through his hands and feet. When he was lifted up in the heat of the morning sun, he became like a holy whirlwind drawing into himself all of the sins of the world, all of our pride and greed, hate and lust, all of our tendencies to hurt one another, all of our lies, gossip, domination and violence. King Jesus took all of our sin. He took every act of bullying, body shaming, every harsh word ever spoken—words like "You're not pretty enough. You're not skinny enough. You are not smart enough. You are not good enough." He took every act of verbal, physical, emotional, and sexual abuse. King Jesus took it all.

He took not only our personal sins, but he also took away all the big systems of sin: poverty, epidemic sickness, economic inequality, racial superiority, exploitation, war, terrorism, environmental degradation, and political corruption—all of our racism, sexism, and classism, all of those things that tear us apart. King Jesus took into his flesh all that destroys human flourishing. Jesus tasted it and swallowed it whole, responding with words of forgiveness on his lips. He takes it away for our salvation and at the same time reveals the very nature of God in an ultimate way. The God of creation, the God of Israel, the God whom King Jesus called Father is cruciform (that is, cross-shaped), self-giving and co-suffering love. This God looks like Jesus on the cross.

A CROSS-SHAPED PEOPLE

Going to the cross is how Jesus became King. Taking up the cross is how we live in that kingdom. The cross shows us what God is like and the cross shows us who we can be. God is cruciform and by faith so are we. King Jesus takes our sin into the grave so we can live free in God's good world. With sin and death defeated, we are drawn into a new world, where we live in imitation of the one who loved us and gave up his life for us. We are called, as Jesus taught us, to take up our cross as an act of self-denial and follow him (Mark

8:34). We are called to be the cruciform people of God in the broken-down world where the new creation has begun to blossom. At the cross Jesus took away our sins, for "he himself bore our sins in his body on the tree, that we might die to sin and live to righteousness" (1 Peter 2:24). His woundedness has brought us healing, but the way of the cross does not end with experiencing God's healing work in our hearts and in our bodies. The way of the cross also provides a way for us to live. "Christ also suffered for you, leaving you an example, so that you might follow in his steps" (1 Peter 2:21). The way of the cross includes the way of vulnerability, opening one's self up to ourselves and others.

To follow in Jesus' steps doesn't mean we should go looking for suffering. It doesn't mean we irresponsibly put ourselves in harmful situations or allow people to hurt us unmercifully. On more than one occasion Jesus avoided suffering by slipping through the midst of an angry crowd or departing to a lonely place to pray. One time Jesus even hid himself to avoid being pummeled to death by stones (John 8:59). The way of the cross isn't the means by which oppressors are allowed to oppress and bullies are allowed to push people around forever, because Jesus comes to rescue both the oppressed and the oppressor. Jesus wants to save both the downtrodden and the bully.

Weakness and vulnerability in the way of the cross does not look like silence in the light of injustice. Rather, it resembles an active resistance to striking back when we are stricken down and resisting the infliction of pain on the one who hurt us so deeply. This anti-retaliatory sentiment was known by the first disciples commissioned by Jesus. As Sean Palmer described it, "Jesus sends his first disciples out like lambs among wolves, armed only with vulnerability."[4] The risk of vulnerability is the way of the cross. For the first ten years of marriage I thought that to love my wife sacrificially like Christ loved the church meant that I never expressed to my wife when I was hurt or when I felt frustrated with her. My failed attempts of "being tough" and never expressing how I felt caused me to build up animosity and resentment. I had to learn that sacrificial love required transparency, a willingness to vocalize what I was feeling. Vulnerability isn't silent. As cross-shaped people we live with an others-first orientation, but we don't attempt to shut down and suppress feelings of anger, disappointment, and woundedness.

All human suffering is relative to a specific time and place in a specific culture. We don't need to judge one another or compare our suffering to the suffering of others who live in a different place or at a different time. Christians who lived during the first couple of centuries under the oppression of the Roman Empire suffered differently than those living in modern-day empires. Those suffering today in certain Muslim-majority countries suffer differently than those living in North America. We only know our suffering subjectively. The suffering we all share in the way of the cross is the temporary suffering of delayed gratification. We choose to say no today to certain pleasures, because patience is our guide in the cruciform life. We are learning to wait with King Jesus because we believe our "light momentary affliction is preparing for us an eternal weight of glory beyond all comparison" (2 Corinthians 4:17). We say no today, because we believe we will receive a greater reward in the future. We were once poisoned by the fruit of sinful nature, but now in Christ as we take up our cross we are transformed into being more like Jesus so we can bear the fruit of the Spirit.

This way of the cross is certainly the way of finding our true selves—the way of finding who we are supposed to be—but it is not the way for getting in touch with our inner desires and being "authentic." Radical authenticity is the mistaken task of being true to ourselves and determining what seems natural to us, though we are still sick with sin. This kind of authenticity rejects all outside influences, conventions, and moral knowledge. Being "true to yourself" enthrones the false self and follows the self's royal decrees, justifying this as "spontaneity," "freedom," and "being who I am." When Jesus told his disciples, "If anyone would come after me, let him deny himself and take up his cross daily and follow me," they understood the meaning of the metaphor (Luke 9:23). Our old selves, incapacitated with sickness and the decay of death, need to die so we can rise with King Jesus and find our true selves. God is love, and God loves us with an affection we struggle to comprehend. God created each of us to be a unique image bearer of God. But we do not find our true selves by looking inward at every desire and inclination of our hearts. We all want to be our true selves as created by God, but we have to be honest with the lingering effects of the soul sickness we have all experienced. You have heard it said, "To thine own self be true." But I say to you, "*What if you're a jerk?*" People could argue that they were born that way or that they were formed in the way of brutality and hostility. While that may be true, it would be a false assumption to think they have to stay that way. Jesus calls us to *come* as we are, but he does not intend for us to *stay* as we are.

As a cross-shaped people we choose humility, which is no more celebrated as a virtue today than in the days of Jesus and the disciples. Shaped by Greek influences, the Roman Empire touted the powers of the mind and human reason. Humility is a lowly state of mind. It isn't a matter of self-loathing or self-hatred. Rather, humility is a healthy skepticism of our own point of view. As it has been said, "Humility is not thinking less of yourself; it is thinking of yourself less."[5] To be humble in the way of the cross is to be humble like Jesus was. In that early hymn of the church, Paul writes, Christ Jesus, "though he was in the form of God, did not count equality with God a thing to be grasped, but emptied himself, by taking the form of a servant, being born in the likeness of men. And being found in human form, he humbled himself by becoming obedient to the point of death, even death on a cross" (Philippians 2:6-8). Jesus humbled himself in his descent from heaven to earth. It took humility for Jesus to empty himself, laying aside his power and authority as God to become a human being. Jesus further humbled himself as he continued his descent from humanity into *suffering* humanity. He suffered, not because he was thinking primarily about himself, but because he was thinking about God's promises to rescue a world gone wrong as he prayed, "Father forgive them . . ." (Luke 23:34). He died to demonstrate God's faithfulness to the promise he made to Abraham's people: that God would have one multicultural family made up of all the peoples of the earth.

CHANGING THE WORLD

God not only wants to rescue individuals, God wants to rescue the world. That is, God wants to rescue the current arrangement of society. God could have chosen to save the world in an infinite number of ways, but he chose to save the world through his image-bearing creatures. The answer to the corruption we see in Genesis 3–11 is the covenant God formed with Abraham. Jesus came to demonstrate God's faithfulness to the covenant, to indeed bless all the families of the earth through the descendants of Abraham. This blessing and salvation for the entire world comes through us who have been grafted into the people of God so that the blessing and the vocation of Abraham may come upon the Gentiles (Galatians 3:14).

The Epistle of Mathetes to Diognetus is a late second-century Christian letter of unknown origins. It can help as we seek to walk in the way of the cross and be the people through whom God changes the world. The early Christian author wrote, "Christians do not live apart in separate cities of their own, speak any special dialect, nor practice any eccentric way of life. . . . Nevertheless, the organization of their community does exhibit some features that are remarkable, and even surprising. . . . They show love to all men and all men persecute them. They are misunderstood, and condemned; yet by suffering death they are quickened into life."[6]

The way of the cross is not merely a matter of what we eat or how we dress. The way of the cross cannot be summed up by a long list of stringent rules, even as, we will discover, some rules are necessary. What marks us as a cruciform people is the way we love.

God is changing people one life at a time as we live as a people of self-giving, co-suffering love in the way of the cross. In doing so we become to the world what the soul is to the body. We become the life-giving air people breathe as others choke on the pollution of power, greed, and corruption. This commitment to be the cruciform people of God in the world was the triumph of the civil rights movement in the 1960s. In his "A Christmas Sermon on Peace," preached in 1967, Martin

Luther King Jr. uttered these words: "I've seen too much hate to want to hate, myself, and every time I see it, I say to myself, hate is too great a burden to bear. Somehow we must be able to stand up against our most bitter opponents and say: 'We shall match your capacity to inflict suffering by our capacity to endure suffering. We will meet your physical force with soul force. Do to us what you will and we will still love you.'"[7] Taking a stand for "godly principles" isn't going to change the world. Our angry rhetoric isn't going to change much of anything. Only the outstretched arms of a cruciform people give the world a chance to see real change.

discussion **questions**

1. What do you do to express your faith in public?

2. In what ways does the cross of Jesus demonstrate the presence of the kingdom of God?

3. How have you seen sin as a drawing away from love?

4. What does it mean to believe Jesus takes away our sin at the cross?

5. How does the cross show us what God is like?

6. What does Christian vulnerability look like?

7. Do you consider yourself a patient person? What does delayed gratification look like for you?

8. How do you see God rescuing the world through Christians who look like Jesus?

9. What do you need to do this week to grow in the way of the cross?

4

Life
The Way of Resurrection

I can almost feel the eerie stillness when I imagine the sealed tomb of Jesus blanketed in darkness. The air must have been unmistakably still as those who loved Jesus and knew him best entered into a time of mourning and grief. Jesus told his traveling companions, his closest followers, that he would be rejected and killed, but on the third day he would be raised. But they simply did not understand. How could they? People of the first-century world had little imagination for resurrection. Sure, Jesus had raised a handful of people from the dead, but now he himself was dead. The religious and political authorities had formed an unholy alliance to kill Jesus. They were successful. As Jesus gasped for his last few breaths he uttered, "It is finished." Then he died. With his seemingly premature death all of the hopes for Jewish liberation and the coming of God's kingdom died in the hearts and minds of those who sacrificed everything to follow Jesus. This was the first day.

Joseph of Arimathea and Nicodemus took down Jesus' body and laid it in a garden tomb before sundown because it was the beginning of the Jewish Sabbath. The next day the lifeless body of the Son of God, wrapped with strips of linen and covered with spices in preparation for decay, lay motionless on a cold rock slab. Then the sun went down on the tomb. The darkness of that night served to amplify the despondency of all the followers of Jesus. "We had hoped that he was the one to redeem Israel," a believer in Jesus would say later (Luke 24:21). The brightness that came with all of Jesus' words, all of his miracles, and all his fearless confrontations with the religious hypocrisy of his day was now swallowed up in a black hole of despair. Jesus, whom many believed to be Israel's Messiah and Savior of the world, was now dead. This was the second day.

Then came the promised third day. Before dawn, as the ominous darkness lingered on, Mary Magdalene came to the tomb according to John's gospel. She loved Jesus and wanted to honor him in his death. As she approached the place where he was buried, she encountered the most unexpected thing. The stone had been rolled back from the entrance to the tomb. She must have squinted and rubbed the sleep out of her eyes to take a second look. But yes, it was true. Someone must have taken the body of Jesus because the tomb was empty! Mary didn't hesitate. She didn't find a rock upon which to sit down and weep. Mary ran. She summoned all the energy she could muster and darted down the road to tell Peter and John.

Upon hearing this shocking news, the three of them returned to the tomb in a mad dash. The two men saw the empty tomb, but they didn't understand what had happened. They walked away bewildered. When the rush of shock and confusion wore off, tears finally did come to Mary's eyes. She cried from a place of deep anguish and through her tears she looked again into the tomb and there she saw an angel. Turning back around she saw a man who she assumed was the gardener arriving early in the morning to tend the grounds around the tomb. When the man said her name, she knew it was Jesus! She wanted to embrace him, but Jesus sent her with an urgent mission: to tell the disciples that he was risen. With this command from the risen Jesus, Mary of Magdala, an insignificant woman with a troubled past, became the first preacher of the Easter message.

A NEW WORLD

The resurrection of Jesus was the first sign that the light of God's new world had permeated the darkness of the old world. God was doing something new, just as the Jewish prophets had said. Hosea saw a coming day when God would make a new covenant of peace and security, a new day when God says, "I will abolish the bow, the sword, and war from the land, and I will make you lie down in safety" (Hosea 2:18). Isaiah brought comfort to the Jewish exiles by announcing the coming of Israel's God, a time when "every valley shall be lifted up, and every mountain and hill be made low; the uneven ground shall become level, and the rough places a plain. And the glory of the Lord shall be revealed" (Isaiah 40:4-5). Jeremiah saw the coming of a new covenant for God's new world when God says, "I will put my law within them, and I will write it on their hearts. And I will be their God, and they shall be my people. And no longer shall each one teach his neighbor and each his brother, saying, 'Know the Lord,' for they shall all know me, from the least of them to the greatest, declares the Lord. For I will forgive their iniquity, and I will remember their sin no more" (Jeremiah 31:33-34). Micah saw the day when the house of the Lord would be lifted up like a high mountain "and many nations shall come, and say: 'Come, let us go up to the mountain of the Lord, to the house of the God of Jacob, that he may teach us his ways and that we may walk in his paths'" (Micah 4:2).

Daniel saw a vision of a coming kingdom that wouldn't be like any of the kingdoms the world had seen. This kingdom would never be defeated or dismantled. In Daniel's vision, "There came one like a son of man, and he came to the Ancient of Days and was presented before him. And to him was given dominion and glory and a kingdom, that all peoples, nations, and languages should serve him; his dominion is an everlasting dominion, which shall not pass away, and his kingdom one that shall not be destroyed" (Daniel 7:13-14). Zechariah saw living water flowing from Jerusalem and covering the earth with a cleansing flood—"and the Lord will be king over all the earth" (Zechariah 14:9). Jesus had conquered death, and the resurrection stood as an immovable kingdom sign of the triumph of life over death, love over dominance, and justice over exploitation. Jesus is alive and with his resurrection we find a new world of peace with Jesus ruling as King of the earth.

As central as the cross is to our faith, the story of Jesus isn't complete without the resurrection. We root our hope of salvation in the resurrection of Jesus. "If Christ has not been raised, your faith is futile and you are still in your sins. Then those also who have fallen asleep in Christ have perished. If in Christ we have hope in this life only, we are of all people most to be pitied" (1 Corinthians 15:17-19). Jesus came to rescue us from our sins not as the currency in a transaction between God and humanity, but as the embodied presence of a new kind of humanity. We aren't saved to go to heaven upon death, as hopeful as that is. We are saved so that we can live new human lives as citizens following Jesus in God's new world here on earth. As N. T. Wright observed, "The point of the resurrection is the reaffirmation of the divine plan for the human race. Resurrected humanity, it seems, is humanity reaching its full goal."[1] The resurrection of Jesus removed the fear and sting of death, enabling us to live in God's new world as a new kind of humanity.

The ancient world hadn't seen anything quite like the resurrection of Jesus. In the ancient world people knew the stories of ghosts coming back from the grave. But no one in the world of ancient Greece or Rome took those stories to be historical fact. They passed them on as myths and legends because no one was making the claim that dead people came alive in bodily form. Many Jewish people believed there would be a resurrection of the dead at the end of the age whereby the God of creation would dismantle death itself and cause the dead to live again. When Jesus talked to Martha after the death of her brother Lazarus, Jesus offered hope by telling Martha he would rise again. She responded, "I know that he will rise again in the resurrection on the last day" (John 11:24). She expressed a common Jewish belief in a final resurrection of the dead, but Jesus offered her more than that by replying in words that she could hardly understand, but words she believed. Jesus said to her, "I am the resurrection and the life. Whoever believes in me, though he die, yet shall he live, and everyone who lives and believes in me shall never die. Do you believe this?" (John 11:25-26). Neither Jews nor Gentiles had any way to imagine that a person who was dead could come back to real physical life. And then Jesus started raising the dead. The raising of Lazarus demonstrated what Jesus meant when he said, "I am the resurrection and the life." Jesus came to defeat sin and death on our behalf through his death and resurrection. He died on a Friday and he rose on a Sunday. Sorrow endures for the night but joy comes in the morning! The Orthodox Church celebrates the resurrection with these words: "Christ is risen from the dead, trampling down death by death and on those in the tomb bestowing life."[2] Jesus tasted death so that he could swallow it whole; those who believe in him, even though they die, yet shall they live.

PRACTICE RESURRECTION

With death's stinger removed, we come alive and find ourselves free to explore God's new world. We believe deeply in our hearts that God raised Jesus from the dead, but God offers resurrection not only as a doctrine to be believed but as a reality to be lived. We not only believe in the resurrection, we practice it. We walk in the way of resurrection to discover real life. The doorway into resurrection life is baptism. "Do you not know that all of us who have been baptized into Christ Jesus were baptized into his death? We were buried therefore with him by baptism into death, in order that, just as Christ was raised from the dead by the glory of the Father, *we too might walk in newness of life*" (Romans 6:3-4, emphasis mine). Baptism is our Red Sea crossing. God has taken us out of Egypt with its slavery and bondage to sin and has led us to the Promised Land, a land flowing with milk and honey, a life of love and light. Through baptism we formally and officially join the people of God as members of God's covenant family.

When we are plunged below the waters of baptism, or when water is poured on our head, we are mystically baptized into the death of Jesus. The water becomes for us a grave where we die to our old life and our false self. When we come up out of the water (or rise up from our knees), we rise into the newness of Jesus' own resurrection. We enter God's new world, but change comes slowly. We don't automatically change into a different person, but baptism offers us the first glimpse of seeing both the world and ourselves in a new way. We come through the water into a new family as citizens of God's new world with a new identity. We are cross-shaped people. We are resurrection people walking in newness of life in the ways of Jesus.

We rise into this new life and experience forgiveness not only to have a personal relationship with Jesus and go to heaven when we die. We rise with him so that we can live in our new identity and walk in a new life. We are united with Jesus and thus we have a relationship with him, a relationship we will learn to cultivate through prayer and worship. But God gives us an experience of new life so we can walk in the way of resurrection life. Jesus died and rose from the dead to *forgive* us of our sins, *free* us from our slavery, and *fortify* us to walk in newness of life. Through Jesus' resurrection we are learning to walk in his ways, just as Micah said.[3] The ways of God's new world are the ways of the kingdom of God. One of the songs the Jewish people would sing as they traveled to Jerusalem for one of their festivals speaks of a blessing bestowed on those who not only fear God in awe and respect, but on the person "who walks in his ways" (Psalm 128:1). As God's people walking in the way of resurrection we are invited by God's Spirit to walk in God's ways.

As resurrection people we don't just believe certain things about Jesus; we practice particular things in the way of Jesus. This value of doing Jesus things underscores the instructions to the church in Philippi to do more than learn, receive, and listen: "What you have learned and received and heard and seen in me—practice these things, and the God of peace will be with you" (Philippians 4:9). As years have become decades in my journey of following Jesus, I have identified four essential practices that have guided me in the way of resurrection life: awareness, learning, reflecting, and action.[4] These four practices open the door to all the other practices of the faith. When we adopt these four practices, the way of life opens up for us.

AWARENESS

The first of the four practices begins with a rather counterintuitive and passive practice—awareness. It's doing by not doing. We live in a high-tech, digital, fast-paced modern society which allows us to constantly do more. It's a world structured to reward accomplishment and production. Jesus calls us out of the madness of the modern world into God's new world where our value is found more in who we are than in what we do. Following Jesus into this resurrection country begins by slowing down for a moment, taking a deep breath, and, in the words of Brother Lawrence, practicing the presence of God. For Brother Lawrence, a seventeenth-century monk, our connectivity to the God who made us isn't restricted to what we would call "religious activities." Rather, he advocated for a regular practice of awareness and attentiveness, "a realization of the presence of God, which can be brought about either by the imagination or by understanding."[5]

We are following Jesus into a God-saturated world. God isn't distant or far away, but is intimately connected to the world God created. We often think of God popping into our lives and doing what only God can do and then returning to heaven. We pray and ask for God's help. We sense God's peace and then go on about our day. But have you stopped and considered that God doesn't just enter our world momentarily and then vanish?

Have you ever considered the reality that our entire world participates in the life of God? I enjoy running in wooded areas either on a trail or through our historic neighborhood lined with massive, aged, mature trees. One of my favorite things to do is to go on multi-day backpacking trips where I spend hours upon hours walking through the woods. In moments of running or hiking when I look at the variety of trees—pines, oaks, maples, and others—supported by thick trunks with branches reaching up into the sky over my head, I think to myself, "These trees are stretching out into the presence of God." The clouds above me are moving along through the presence of God. Think about it for a moment. God is quite literally everywhere, and everything lives and moves in God's presence. In every molecule of oxygen you are breathing, in the very place where you're sitting, in this book you are holding, all of it is participating in the presence of God. We look in vain when we search for God within this life, because God is the substance of life itself. God isn't an object in what we know as reality. God is the essence of reality itself.

During my freshman year of college, I took a required oral communications class. I had full intentions of becoming a pastor at the time. Excitement overwhelmed me when our professor said we would deliver various speeches to our

classmates for a grade. I took every opportunity in that class
to talk about Jesus. When we had to give a speech about a
historical figure we admired, I delivered a speech about Jesus,
quoting not only from the Gospels, but from Josephus the
Jewish historian. When asked to deliver a persuasive speech,
I preached the gospel! When asked to present an instruc-
tional speech, I talked about how to respond to the gospel
and become a Christian.

I had the opportunity to talk to a classmate after class one
day about my faith. His name was Joe, a curious and engaging fellow college freshman. Intelligent and articulate, he
claimed to be a seeker, but never considered himself religious.
He called himself an atheist, but he was open to the idea of
"something out there," perhaps a transcendent being or higher
power. At the end of the semester we were all required to offer
a final speech on a topic of our choosing. Of course I chose
to talk about Jesus. Joe used his final opportunity to tell a
story about his first trip to Niagara Falls. He described the
long drive to the falls and how he arrived there at night. He
shared in great detail how he pulled into a parking spot at the
falls and heard the roar as he walked up to see the rushing
water. He then looked at me when he said, "When I turned
the corner and saw the falls illuminated against the dark sky,
it took my breath away. It was the closest thing to God I had
ever experienced." I ran up to him after class with my heart
pounding. "Yes!" I exclaimed. "Yes that was God you experienced because God has made his invisible attributes known in
all creation!" All I knew to do at that time was to quote from
Romans 1:20. Today I would tell Joe that those magnificent
falls are joining with all creation in praising the very presence
of God in our world.

When we practice awareness, we are awake, moment by moment, to the activity of God. We have to work hard at slowing down to be open to God's presence, because everything around us is communicating in subtle (and at times quite explicit) ways that God is absent. The technical term for this message is secularism and it's one of the predominate messages in North America today. Secularism is in the air we breathe. We cannot get away from it. The secular way is any and all attempts to do life without God. The most fundamental thing we can do to resist secularism is to pray, which we will explore in more detail in chapter 9. Prayer is more about growing in awareness of God than it is about the words we speak. The practice of prayer is first and foremost about carving out time and space to be aware of God's presence. Prayer is the least secular thing we do. It's our active resistance to the growing flood waters of secularism that seek to sweep us away. When we pray, we pause to acknowledge the presence of God. Awareness is an ongoing conscious reminder that what is most true about us, the most fundamental thing about us, cannot always be perceived by our five physical senses.

LEARNING

When Jesus invites us to come and follow him, he doesn't require us to go to school first, which is a relief to a lot of people. I went to school for a long time—college, seminary, and doctoral work—so I naturally gravitate toward the learning involved in Christian discipleship. But living as a disciple isn't the same thing as entering into a degree program, or, God forbid, going back to middle school. Certainly we do need to grow in knowledge, but learning in the way of the resurrection is also growing in wisdom. You can accumulate a lifetime of book-learning and never walk in the ways of Jesus. Knowledge and wisdom belong together and we seek after both as followers of Jesus, and our growth in knowledge and wisdom will never surpass our desire for them.

Knowledge is the possession of information. Christians have nothing to gain by remaining blissfully ignorant or boasting in "facts" that aren't based on accurate information. The pursuit of knowledge is a noble endeavor. In fact, when Jesus calls us to him, he calls us to learn from him. Jesus said, "Come to me, all who labor and are heavy laden, and I will give you rest. Take my yoke upon you, and learn from me" (Matthew 11:28-29). We discover we have much to learn in God's new world, because the resurrection of Jesus is like the rising of the sun. We have lived for too long in the darkness of night, navigating by the light of the moon. The brightness of Jesus reveals new things to be learned at the dawn of every new day.

Wisdom is knowing what to do with the knowledge we have. Wisdom determines the direction of our lives and so much of the outcome of our decisions, which is why Proverbs encourages us to "Get wisdom, and whatever you get, get insight. Prize her highly, and she will exalt you" (Proverbs 4:7-8). I'm convinced we will learn the ways of Jesus either through suffering or wisdom. We will learn either by listening to wise people and heeding their advice or by suffering through our own failure. Some suffering is inevitable. As followers of Jesus who take up the cross, we acknowledge our willingness to suffer in obedience to Jesus. This suffering comes to us from the outside. Other kinds of suffering come as the result of our own stubbornness and foolishness. We can avoid this kind of suffering. If knowledge is knowing the length of the desert, then wisdom is making the decision to carry ample water with you as you walk through it.

As we grow in knowledge and wisdom in the way of resurrection we learn how to speak the language of the Christian faith. Adding new words to our vocabulary opens up new ways of thinking. The way of Jesus requires learning the vocabulary of Jesus. As we continue to explore various aspects of the Christian faith we come to learn the meaning of words like *Trinity*, *salvation*, *grace*, *righteousness*, and *ministry*. One of the key words in the Christian vocabulary is the word *incarnation*, which describes the pivotal moment when God became a human being. God's saving plan in Jesus began with his birth in Bethlehem. Through his birth, God raised the dignity of all human flesh by becoming a real human being. All of this understanding and much more is contained in the one word: *incarnation*.

Learning new things implies unlearning old things. In the words of Master Yoda to Luke Skywalker in *The Empire Strikes Back*, "You must unlearn what you have learned." We all come to the Christian faith with preconceived ideas about God, truth, morality, race, sexuality, politics, and faith. Sometimes these ideas are hidden assumptions lodged in the back regions of our minds, held with unquestionable certainty. Some of these ideas are wrong. The admission that we may have some unlearning to do is frightening for some. But it can equally be freeing to admit that none of us have it all figured out. None of us have understood God and the ways of Jesus perfectly, regardless of the length of time we have spent following Jesus. Admitting we don't have all the answers and have more to learn or unlearn is liberating; but between learning and unlearning, unlearning is the hardest part.

Don't abandon the faith when you are in a season of unlearning. Nobody has perfect knowledge of God. We remain lifelong learners because there are always new things to discover. Stay curious. People who remain curious will persist as lifelong learners. Let your learning be led by both your head and your heart. God isn't an academic subject to be studied. God is a person to be encountered, experienced, and loved. Learning in the way of resurrection begins and ends with love. Loving God is ultimately how we know God. Loving Jesus is ultimately how we know the ways of Jesus. We cannot stand at an emotional distance from Jesus as detached investigators. Learning from Jesus requires that we jump in with both feet and love the Jesus who is teaching us.

REFLECTING

Experience itself isn't the best teacher; experience *reflected upon* is. We all go through life having experiences both noteworthy and commonplace. We can classify learning as an experience but the full benefit of learning comes from thinking about what we are learning. There will be more on thinking clearly and Christianly in chapter 6. God didn't create us to be robotic collectors of data, but with the ability to think about the knowledge we have received so that knowledge can give birth to wisdom. Reflection in the way of resurrection life requires mental energy, but it's more than classifying facts in our brains. Reflection is rooted in awareness and learning. It's thinking in the presence of God. It's thinking in Christ.

Reflection comes to our aid when we are learning new things and doing the hard work of unlearning. When we are confronted by Jesus with something new—a new perspective or a new way of thinking—the worst thing we can do is reject it. When we feel challenged by Jesus to consider something new and it begins to create anxiety within us, we need to slow down and ask ourselves questions like: *Where is this anxiety coming from? What am I afraid of? How is this new idea connected to what I already know about Jesus and the Jesus way? What is this new idea asking of me? What do I need to give up? What do I need to change?* Don't merely absorb information. Rather, work things through in your mind and try to connect the dots. Immature people assume they know it all and understand everything perfectly. I know for myself, I had it all figured out when I was eighteen years old. Or at least I thought I did! I grew in the way of resurrection by reflecting. I am still learning and growing, but I have practiced a reflected openness which has brought maturity to my thinking.

Journaling is a helpful practice for some. Write your reflections down because as Flannery O'Connor was reported to say, "I write because I don't know what I think until I read what I say." Sometimes we do not know what we think until we read what we wrote. Writing provides a helpful way to reflect. Thinking is good, but don't do the work of reflecting alone. Think aloud with friends who are also following Jesus. Talk through what you are reflecting upon and allow them to ask you questions and invite them to offer insight to help in the process. Learn to think with Jesus. Learn to sit in the presence of Jesus with what you are learning and be open to the surprising work of God. The great Christian tradition calls this contemplation. Thinking is what we do with our rational self. Contemplation is what we do with our spiritual self. We need both.

ACTION

Walking in newness of life in step with Jesus requires movement. Following Jesus looks much more like hiking in the woods than sitting in a classroom. We are aware. We are learning. We have reflected upon what we have learned. Now is the time for action. The first three resurrection practices (awareness, learning, and reflecting) are not complete until we put into action what we have discovered. We are aware so we can become animated. We are learning so we can live. We are reflecting so we can respond. Jesus said, "If you love me, you will keep my commandments" (John 14:15). In other words, if we say we love Jesus then we will do what he says, because all of Christ's commands are rooted in our best intentions. All four practices are necessary, but action is fundamental. Following Jesus doesn't become a living way until we begin to put into motion what we have been thinking about and learning; the way of resurrection necessitates a change in our behavior. We are sons and daughters who have come alive in the light of God's love and we live, not as people of the darkness, but as people of the light. This action flows from hearts that have been changed as we are empowered and transformed by the Holy Spirit.

These four practices, culminating with action, can be used as we climb all the mountains of the Christian faith. One of the highest peaks is forgiveness. Jesus taught us to forgive others as we have been forgiven. We are taught to pray for forgiveness as we forgive those who have sinned against us. Jesus teaches forgiveness with this warning, "If you forgive others their trespasses, your heavenly Father will also forgive you, but if you do not forgive others their trespasses, neither will your Father forgive your trespasses" (Matthew 6:14-15). Jesus is teaching us God's activity in forgiveness. As we follow Jesus we learn that we don't just forgive seven times but seventy times seven times. Jesus doesn't mean that we have to forgive 490 times. Rather he is reversing Lamech's revenge. Lamech declared after killing a man that "if Cain's revenge is seven-fold, then Lamech's is seventy-sevenfold" (Genesis 4:24). Jesus flipped Lamech's declaration upside down. In Jesus' kingdom, forgiveness, not revenge, would be multiplied. In learning this high-reaching value as followers of Jesus, we have to reflect on those who have hurt us. How should we respond? We have to sit with Jesus with the pain caused by those who have hurt us. Now what? Now we have to go and forgive!

These four practices in the way of resurrection have a natural progression from one practice to the next, but they are intended to be a cycle. Action leads to a greater sense of awareness of the presence of God. We never exhaust the knowledge of God. In fact, the more we know, the more we become aware of what we don't know. The cycle never really ends. The way of resurrection hasn't been given to us so we would know all the answers, but that we would follow Jesus into the adventure of knowing God and being fully known by God. The four practices serve as gear in our backpacks as we embark on the lifelong adventure of following Jesus who has risen from the dead. The way of resurrection provides for us the way to true life. The four practices provide us with an ongoing guide as we explore God's new world, a world experienced by love.

discussion **questions**

1. What Easter traditions did you practice as a child? What do you continue to practice today?

2. How does the resurrection of Jesus confirm God's commitment to creation and humanity?

3. What kind of change, if any, did you see in your life after your baptism?

4. What was one of the first things you started doing when you first became a Christian?

5. How does your awareness of God change, knowing all creation participates in the life of God?

6. In three words how would you describe God's new world?

7. We don't all learn in the same way. How do you learn best?

8. What is one thing you have unlearned as a follower of Jesus? Was it easy or hard to unlearn it?

9. When you are working to figure things out, how do you do your best thinking? Talking out loud to another person? Writing things down? Sitting quietly alone? Something else?

10. What can you do this week to be fully alive in God's new world?

5

Trinity

The Way of Love

Discipleship dances to the beat of love. Intentionally following Jesus with our whole hearts will always lead us in the way of love. We can talk about discipleship, read books about discipleship, and take classes on discipleship. All of these are worthwhile activities. But if we don't love, we haven't crossed the starting line toward the goal of becoming a disciple of Jesus. Be careful not to confuse *knowledge about love* with love. While knowledge gained from reading and classes is helpful, it can sometimes masquerade as love. We can too easily rest in our knowledge of Christian discipleship and unknowingly allow the things we know to form us into arrogant know-it-alls and even cruel people. Our knowledge should be saturated with love so that we love what we learn and learn in order to love. As Karl Rahner puts it, "In the heart

of knowledge stands love, from which knowledge itself lives."[1]
If we are devoid of love, knowledge means very little. As Paul
remarked, "If I . . . understand all mysteries and all knowledge,
and if I have all faith, so as to remove mountains, but have not
love, I am nothing" (1 Corinthians 13:2). From the beginning
with Jesus' bold announcement of the presence of the kingdom of God, the road leading to life has been paved with love.

Jesus told his followers then, and he is telling us now, "A
new commandment I give to you, that you love one another:
just as I have loved you, you also are to love one another.
By this all people will know that you are my disciples, if you
have love for one another" (John 13:34-35). Jesus gave us
love as the defining mark of discipleship. People looking in
from the outside will know we are followers of Jesus by the
way we love one another. Remember who was in that group
when Jesus spoke these words. Among Jesus' original twelve
disciples were Simon the Zealot and Matthew the tax collec-
tor. These two guys came from opposite ends of the political spectrum in first-century Jewish life. Zealots were Jewish
nationalists ready to restore Jewish civic dominance and expel
the Romans by violent force. Tax collectors were Jewish sell-
outs, out to make money for themselves by working for the
dreaded Roman Empire. In our world this would be like a
hard-right Republican and a far-left Democrat both attempt-
ing to follow Jesus and hearing Jesus tell them to join hands
and love one another. The Zealots and tax collectors in Jesus'
day shared nearly nothing in common and they held a gut-
level, smoldering disdain for one another. But Jesus told Simon
the nationalist and Matthew the sellout that if they could put
aside their political opinions and love one another with sincere
brotherly affection, then the world would know they were

followers of Jesus. Admittedly, loving people who are not like us is a challenge.

At first look, following Jesus in the way of love seems easy enough, because we all think we know what we mean when we say, "We love . . ." But we have a problem. We have a deficiency in the English language in that we only have one word for "love." We love our cars. We love our jobs (most of the time). We love our kids, our spouses, and our fathers and mothers. We love our favorite sports teams. We love chocolate ice cream. We love our dogs and cats. We say we love all these things and people, but these are not the same kind of love. (Be honest if you are married: you don't really love your spouse in the same way you love your mom!) We use the same word to mean different kinds of things. The ancient Greeks had different words for love. They used the word *eros* to describe romantic or sexual love, *philos* to describe friendship or fraternal love, and *agape* to describe self-giving love. In English we have one word to communicate all three. So when Jesus calls us to love one another, what kind of love is this?

DEFINING JESUS' LOVE

Jesus invites us to join him in the way of loving one another as the outworking of our love for God. The greatest commandment, according to Jesus, is rooted in an ancient Jewish prayer: "And you shall love the Lord your God with all your heart and with all your soul and with all your mind and with all your strength" (Mark 12:30). We love the one true God of creation, the God of Israel, the God and Father of our Lord Jesus, with both intentionality and action. We love God by giving attention to God and we express that love by loving our neighbor, loving our enemies, and loving one another in the family of

God. We begin to grasp what it means to love one another in the light of loving God, but the question remains: *What kind of love is this?*

We clarify our love for God by understanding who God is. God *is* love. John, one of Jesus' original disciples, had the opportunity to experience Jesus up close and face-to-face. John communicated to us what he heard, saw, and touched with his hands. He writes, "So we have come to know and to believe the love that God has for us. God is love, and whoever abides in love abides in God, and God abides in him" (1 John 4:16). Love is what is most fundamental about the essence and nature of the God revealed in Jesus and by the Holy Spirit. God is love without being selfish or self-absorbed. God isn't love because God loves himself. God is love because God is a holy community, the Father, Son, and Holy Spirit who infinitely love one another.[2] The word Christians use to describe the love of God as relational movement is *Trinity*.

While the word *Trinity* never appears in the Bible, our Scriptures are filled with references to the God whom Jesus called Father, references to Jesus himself who claimed to be God's Son, and references to the Spirit who mysteriously proceeds from the Father and the Son. For example, Paul ends his second letter to the church in Corinth with these words: "The grace of the Lord Jesus Christ and the love of God and the fellowship of the Holy Spirit be with you all" (2 Corinthians 13:14). The language of the Trinity is a gift from the ancient church to the modern church. The people who gave us the Bible also gave us the understanding of God as Trinity. The early church received the witness of the apostles as recorded in Scripture that God the Father, Jesus, and the Holy Spirit are united in one divine essence.

As we have seen, we formally begin the process of being made into disciples through baptism, where we are baptized into the trifold name of God. Jesus said, "All authority in heaven and on earth has been given to me. Go therefore and make disciples of all nations, baptizing them in the name of the Father and of the Son and of the Holy Spirit" (Matthew 28:18-19). We are baptized *into* the triune life of God. We don't believe in three gods. We believe in one God who has revealed himself in the Father, Son, and Spirit. According to historian Philip Schaff, "The church teaches not one divine essence *and* three persons, but one essence *in* three persons. Father, Son, and Spirit cannot be conceived as three separate individuals, but are in one another, and form a solidaric unity."[3] The Father is God. The Son is God. The Spirit is God. But the Father is not the Son. The Son is not the Spirit, and the Spirit is not the Father. *This concept of God as Trinity sounds confusing doesn't it?* The Christian belief in the Trinity isn't a mathematical problem to be solved, but a mystery to be explored.

SELF-GIVING TRINITARIAN LOVE

Following Jesus in the way of trinitarian love isn't about figuring out what God is like with logical precision. Rather it's the lifelong joy of exploring the mystery of the God who is unlike anything in all creation. Gregory of Nazianzus from the fourth century described exploring this mystery in terms of undivided light:

> No sooner do I conceive of the One than am I illumined by the Splendor of the Three; no sooner do I distinguish Them than I am carried back to the One. When I think of any One of the Three I think of Him as the Whole, and my

eyes are filled, and the greater part of what I am thinking escapes me. I cannot grasp the greatness of that One so as to attribute a greater greatness to the Rest. When I contemplate the three together, I see but one torch, and cannot divide or measure out the Undivided Light.[4]

The beautiful concept of God as Trinity has been given to us so that we might gaze on the beauty of the Three and the One, to get lost in the flames of an undivided and uncreated light. Think of it like this . . .

God the Father, Son, and Spirit have existed as a holy community since before the beginning of creation. Imagine three people standing in a huddle with their arms on the shoulders of the person on their left and right. Let the unbroken huddle represent the unity of God. Let each person represent the distinctiveness of the three. God as Trinity has existed before time and space, before matter and creation, before light and dark, and before male and female. The Trinity has lived as a community of mutual affection. The Father, Son, and Spirit have existed in a perfect dance of self-giving love. Some people have trouble imagining persons in community who draw their identity from the community because we tend to think of a person in isolation. In our modern world a unique authentic person is an individual. Yet all the members of the Trinity are who they are in relationship to the other members. The Father is who he is in relationship to the Son and the Spirit; this could be said about the Son and Spirit as well.

Within the Trinity, God is immensely happy and eternally focused on loving the other. In creation God opened himself in order to create something not himself. Irenaeus, a second-century church father, described the Son and Spirit as the hands of the Father. God opens up his hands in order to create and fashion a world to be a place where he could dwell. God, who is perfectly content within this dance of love, remains open in order to invite us into the very life of God. So here we are, creatures of the earth minding our own business, doing our own thing, stumbling and fumbling our way through life on our own, while God stands by with welcoming arms spread wide. In opening himself, God the Father has sent his Son, and through the Son he sent his Spirit to invite us to come. Jesus says come. The Spirit says come. All we have to do is stop, turn away from our selfish ways, and turn by faith to the God who is love and come into the life of God where we will be welcomed with love from another world.

What do we see in this vision of the Trinity? More than anything we see God is love. God is love not in theory or abstraction or an idea. God is love in relationship, a love that lives with its focus on the other. According to Darrell Johnson, this love is at the very center of the universe: "The living God is not a solitary God. The living God is not an isolated God. From all eternity the living God has lived in relationship— indeed, has lived as relationship. At the center of the universe is relationship."[5] God is pure love-in-relationship. God isn't a mixture of love and wrath. No hate or anger can be found within the Trinity, because God's essence is love. All we know about God and all of the actions of God in the world flow from this undiluted heart of love. For followers of Jesus, the Trinity is how we define love.

HOLY LOVE

For a long time I struggled to understand the wrath of God. Early in my Christian experience I believed God was both a God of love and of wrath, anger, hate. This understanding of the nature of God shaped how I imagined God viewed me. When I was doing good, God loved me. But when I sinned, when I did something wrong, then God let me see his anger. I had bought into the idea that God was too holy to look upon me in my sin. So in my failure God was wrathful. I felt content with this understanding of God. It's consistent with many Christian traditions. This view also empowers an effective form of discipleship. Obey Jesus or get the wrath of God. It works! It checks all the pragmatic boxes in trying to form people in the ways of Jesus. *But is this the way Jesus has revealed God the Father to us? Is this fear-based view of God true? More importantly is it good and beautiful?*

In the mid-2000s while I was a young pastor, I went through a bit of an identity crisis as a follower of Jesus through a rediscovery of the Trinity. While I had described myself as a charismatic Christian, I had moved on from the narrow confines of the charismatic movement into something more ecumenical. While I embraced the fullness of the Spirit, I began to grow in my love for the whole body of Christ. I found myself reading and being shaped by many different Christian traditions including Orthodoxy, Wesleyanism, Anglicanism, and the Anabaptist tradition. Instead of identifying as a "charismatic," I found it more helpful to call myself a "trinitarian." From that time forward, the preeminence of love as the sole characteristic of God's nature grew brighter and brighter to the point that I now see love not as one attribute among many, but as the essence of who God is. All of the other attributes of God— God's holiness and power, God's mercy and compassion, God's wrath and judgment—flow from who God is. And God is love. According to Colin Gunton, "All God's characteristics are what they are because they are functions of the relations of Father, Son and Spirit in eternity. They are what they are because God is eternally personal love, the love that gives to and receives from the other."[6] God is love plus nothing.

The battle to overcome my fear-based, dualistic understanding of God came to an end while I was reading Brad Jersak's *A More Christlike God*. He writes, "Wrath is a metaphor for the intrinsic consequences of our refusal to live in the mercies of God."[7] In other words, the word *wrath* throughout Scripture is used as a metaphor to point us to the judgment of God which is God's consent to our evil selfish ways. In finishing Jersak's book (in a section entitled "Unwrathing God") I discovered why I struggled so much to accept God as pure and unmixed love. My struggle was rooted in my early theological development as a seminary student.

I remember sitting in my first semester of systematic theology in seminary where our professor described the nature of God. As he lectured, he said we could reduce all the attributes of God down to two words: *holy love*. He wrote those two words on the dry erase board. Then he drew a line between them, extending the line down the board to create two columns like this:

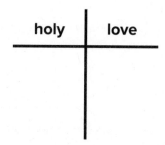

He continued his lecture by listing attributes under each word. Under *holy* he listed things like justice, judgment, anger, wrath, etc. Under *love* he listed things like mercy, grace, compassion, forgiveness, etc. This became an unquestionable framework that would shape how I understood God, how I experienced God, and how I pastored people in the ways of Jesus until my rediscovery of the Trinity.

The two words are an adequate description of the character and nature of God. The problem is the line dividing the two. To attribute things like wrath and anger to God's holiness is simply an artificial connection. Throughout the Scriptures holiness is communicated to us in terms of separateness. God is holy in that God is separate and altogether different from anything else in all creation. God isn't holy because God gets mad. God is holy because God is love and God's love is different than any other kind of love we experience in all creation. References to the "wrath of God" or "anger of God" through our Scriptures are metaphorical pictures of God's judgment. For example, throughout Paul's letter to the Romans the word *wrath* can be replaced with the word *judgment*. Early in the letter, Paul is clear that "wrath" is speaking in a "human way." Paul writes in Romans 3:5, "What shall we say? That God is unrighteous to inflict wrath on us? (I speak in a human way)." The human way is the way of metaphor. Paul is using a human picture of anger (or wrath) and projecting it upon God, so we are alerted to the seriousness of God's judgment. God doesn't literally have anger any more than God has literal eyes or hands. These metaphors are human pictures that communicate very true things to us about God. God doesn't have eyes, but God sees all. God doesn't have hands, but God is at work for all. God doesn't have anger, but God judges all.

God is pure love, a holy and otherworldly kind of love. God is a judge, but his judgment flows from his love, because

God came to save. Jesus himself said, "For God so loved the world, that he gave his only Son, that whoever believes in him should not perish but have eternal life. For God did not send his Son into the world to condemn the world, but in order that the world might be saved through him. Whoever believes in him is not condemned, but whoever does not believe is condemned already, because he has not believed in the name of the only Son of God" (John 3:16-18). Jesus established that it was for love that he came into the world, and further explained that the purpose of his mission was not to condemn but to save.

Jesus didn't come to wipe out God's creation project and start over. Jesus came to restore and repair what had been broken down in the world, including human beings created in God's image. Jesus came to save what had been lost and mend what had been broken. Condemnation, according to Jesus, was already present. Jesus' saving and healing work would include judgment, but God's judgment described by Jesus doesn't look like thunderous lightning bolts from heaven. God's judgment is more like the luminous light of love. Jesus continues, "And this is the judgment: the light has come into the world, and people loved the darkness rather than the light because their works were evil. For everyone who does wicked things hates the light and does not come to the light, lest his works should be exposed" (John 3:19-20). In this sense, "wrath" is what evil looks like when it is exposed by the light of God's love. God wants to save the world, which means God will deal with, and ultimately dismantle, the presence of evil. The wrath of God as a picture of God's judgment is the exposure of evil for what it is, and the painful consequences that follow when we let evil loose in the world.

RESPONDING TO LOVE WITH LOVE

Because God is Trinity, God is a steady never-ending stream of love. God the Father sent Jesus in order to show us this love. Through the Son, the Father pours out the Holy Spirit into the world, and the Son and the Spirit invite us all to come and enter into the love shared between the Father, Son, and Holy Spirit. How we experience that love depends on how we respond to the love of God. If we respond to the love of God with love and acceptance, then we experience salvation. Evangelicalism has a rich tradition of making this appeal clear. We have sinned. Jesus died for our sins in a demonstration of God's love. When we respond to the love of God with love of our own, then we experience that love as grace and forgiveness.

Conversely, if we respond to the love of God with contempt or indifference, then we experience condemnation. Sadly, many experience this kind of condemnation and blame God for it. Many people hear the message of God's grace and they choose to love their evil (which many people refuse to call evil) more than the light of God's love. They run from the light because they don't want their sin to be exposed and shown for what it is. They love the darkness more than the light, so in the darkness of their decisions they suffer the judgment of God. The variable in these two scenarios is our response. The constant is the love of God. The unflinching love of God remains unchanged by human response. God was love. God is love. God will forever be love.

FOUR WAYS TO WALK IN THE WAY OF LOVE

With the Trinity in view we see love in motion. God as Trinity shows us that love is relational. It requires other people. It's self-giving and marked by mutual respect. The love by which we love isn't me-first, but it's the kind of love that redirects our attention to the other. The love overflowing from the Trinity prompts us to action. Here are four ways to walk in the way of love.

1. Prioritize the other. Selfishness saturates the world we live in. The consumer engines that drive our economy have polluted our culture with the toxins of me-first entitlement. From the first day of kindergarten (and perhaps even before then) little Johnny is unwittingly schooled in selfishness. Johnny's lunch box is placed in *his* backpack. He arrives at school and hangs up *his* backpack on the hook identified by *his* name. Johnny promptly finds *his* desk with *his* name on it where he sits down to do *his* work. He selects a pencil from *his* pencil box labeled (again) with *his* name and the first thing he writes on his piece of paper is "Johnny." Perhaps teachers structure kindergarten classes this way because five-year-olds only have the capacity to think primarily of themselves. Maybe. But Johnny's teacher will work hard to convince little Johnny that he has to share the swings at recess.

This example isn't a critique of elementary education so much as it is an example of the world in which we live. Little Johnny grows up to be Mr. Johnny, a middle manager in a dead-end job that he hates. He drinks a bit too much and his small team at work makes fun of him behind his back because they know he only shows up to work for the paycheck. Fortunately the Johnnies of the world don't dominate the workplace, because many people have found other incentives or processes to curtail their self-absorbed ways. Nevertheless our unhealthy preoccupation with ourselves—our drive to satisfy our wants and desires—remains present in our world. Jesus shines the light of his love into this dark place and calls us out. He tells us the greatest of all moral commands is to love God with all we are, and love our neighbor as ourselves. In other words, Jesus calls us to orient our lives and prioritize our loves around love for God and love of neighbor. Indeed we demonstrate our love for God by our love for other people. We do this by prioritizing others over ourselves.

Paul writes to the church in Philippi and encourages them with these words: "If you've gotten anything at all out of following Christ, if his love has made any difference in your life, if being in a community of the Spirit means anything to you, if you have a heart, if you care—then do me a favor: Agree with each other, love each other, be deep-spirited friends. Don't push your way to the front; don't sweet-talk your way to the top. Put yourself aside, and help others get ahead. Don't be obsessed with getting your own advantage. Forget yourselves long enough to lend a helping hand" (Philippians 2:1-4 *The Message*). When we forget about ourselves for a while, then we can go out and see what other people need. When we set aside our self-driven agendas and open ourselves to the other, we can begin to find agreement and respect and to love one another within the Christian family. We walk in the way of love by making space for the other. Of course our love for others has limits. Jesus doesn't require us to continue to prioritize unhealthy or harmful people.

2. Love your enemies. We not only love the people we go to church with and the people in our social circle of friends, we also love our enemies. If you don't have any enemies, think about the people who for whatever reason don't like you. Love them. Our world runs on team-sport animosity where we label our tribe the "good guys" and we label those people over there who are different from us the "bad guys." The antagonism formed between these two groups (and there are innumerable pairs of warring tribes) is the energy fueling so many aspects of our culture. Exhibit A: *Every single presidential election of my lifetime*. I was born under the reign of Richard Nixon, less than two months before his resignation. I was too young to have any memory of Gerald Ford or Jimmy Carter. Ronald Reagan was the first president I can recall from childhood. The presidential campaign of George H. W. Bush was my first taste of political vitriol going back and forth between Republicans and Democrats on issues likes taxes and abortion, mostly ignoring Bush's appeal for a "kinder, gentler nation." For evangelicals of the 1980s who merged their faith in Jesus with a hope in the Republican Party, the Democrats were the enemy. The loss of civility and the increasing nastiness in partisan politics has only grown since then.

Today the antagonism between Republicans and Democrats, elephants and donkeys, has risen as the most visible example of the toxic energy generated by treating the other with contempt. Jesus shows us a better way. Jesus teaches us to love not only people like us, not only people who love us, but people who are different, people we are supposed to be against. Jesus said, "You have heard that it was said, 'You shall love your neighbor and hate your enemy.' But I say to you, Love your enemies and pray for those who persecute you, so that you may be sons of your Father who is in heaven. For he makes his sun rise on the evil and on the good, and sends rain on the just and on the unjust. For if you love those who love you, what reward do you have?" (Matthew 5:43-46). The way of love in following Jesus is the way of tearing down antagonisms and walls that divide. This world without antagonistic walls doesn't mean we will always agree with our enemies.

But we are not called to agree with them; we are called to love them. We love our enemies by setting aside our judgment and listening to them, and working hard to understand where they are coming from. We love them by seeing the world from their perspective. We love them by showing respect, even in the face of disagreement.

3. Reject codependency. Jesus leads us into a life where we love everyone, the freaks and geeks, the lonely and the losers, the outcasts and the obnoxious. We don't choose to love. Rather, as the Spirit continues to form and shape us into the image of Jesus, love becomes an instinct. In this way, love isn't a well-thought-out choice for a mature follower of Jesus. Love is just what we do. Growing in this kind of unconscious love requires the rejection of codependency, because sometimes love says no. Codependency sounds like love and feels like love, but it's a sickness of the soul. According to Robert Hemfelt, Frank Minirth, and Paul Meier it's really an addiction: "In its broadest sense, codependency can be defined as an addiction to people, behaviors or things. Codependency is the fallacy of trying to control interior feelings by controlling people, things, and events on the outside."[8] Codependency uses the language of love between two people, but in actuality, it reflects a relationship that is so enmeshed in an unhealthy singularity that personal responsibility is blurred. The worst kind of codependent relationship exists when one person in the relationship is abusive or struggling with substance abuse.

Over the last two decades of pastoral ministry I have had more than one difficult conversation with a person who has a loved one struggling with drug or alcohol addiction. Once I received a call from a single mom who wanted information about our Celebrate Recovery (CR) ministry. CR is a

Christ-centered twelve-step support ministry offering Christians the tools and encouragement to overcome not only substance abuse, but any of the difficulties of life. This mother had an adult son who was addicted to a variety of drugs. She told me her thirty-five-year-old son regularly did drugs in her home. She said she would do anything to get her son help, but nothing she had tried was working. She wanted to learn more about CR and she was seeking advice. She wanted me to come and talk to her son. She was convinced that if a man, particularly a male pastor, would talk to her son, he would turn his life around and seek help. I politely refused. My experience had proven that a stranger cannot talk addicts into seeking help. The only hope for addicts is for them to hit the proverbial rock bottom where they experience the full weight of the consequences of their actions and then people they know and respect can recommend treatment or participation in a twelve-step program.

I explained to this distraught mother that the best thing she could do was to allow her unemployed son to experience the consequences of his drug use. She had said she tried everything. I asked if she had told him that if he used drugs in her house, he would have to move out. She said she had, but he refused to move out and she could not kick him out. I reminded her that she said she would be willing to do anything. She recanted. There was one thing she wouldn't do. I told her that she could call law enforcement when he was using drugs and they could come arrest him. She said she couldn't do that. In trying to love her son, she had become codependent. Her son was addicted to drugs and she was addicted to him. She became insistent that I come talk to her son. After continuing to refuse, I asked her, "So you want me to come talk to your son hoping that he will follow my advice, but you are unwilling to take the advice I am offering you?" She abruptly ended the conversation. Facing the facts of codependency is tough.

The antidote to codependency can be found in creating emotional boundaries. According to Henry Cloud and John Townsend, "Boundaries define us. They define what is me and what is not me. A boundary shows me where I end and someone else begins, leading me to a sense of ownership."[9] Boundaries are not walls of antagonism. They are clear-cut lines of demarcation that identify who each person is in any given relationship, so that each person in the relationship knows what they are responsible for. This kind of love relationship reflects the Trinity. God is one in God's essence and being, but the oneness of God does not blur out the distinctiveness of the Father, the Son, or the Holy Spirit. Creating emotional and relational boundaries can feel like hate for those who are on the other side of the line. However, it isn't motivated by hate, but by love, allowing both people to understand who they are and what things fall into their area of responsibility. Sometimes love in the way of Jesus means saying no. We say no to the destructive choices and habits of others not to punish them, but to allow them to take responsibility for their actions.

4. Extend mercy. In our desire to follow Jesus we will make mistakes. We need God's mercy, which is why we regularly pray the Jesus Prayer: *Lord Jesus Christ, Son of God, have mercy on me.* The world has only seen one who loves perfectly and we are striving toward that perfection with honest imperfection along the way. We do want to follow Jesus by obeying all his commands, but we will fail at times. People outside of Christ will certainly leave moral flaws in their wake. We don't need to overlook the demands of following Jesus, but in light of all this imperfection we need to share the mercy we have received with others. Mercy flows directly from the love we have received from God. As Colin Gunton observed, "Mercy is the outworking in fallen time and history of the action of a God for whom love of the other is central to his being."[10] God exudes mercy. So should we.

For Christians, the way of love implies that when we don't know what else to do, we love by extending mercy. Love is the answer to all our questions.

What about people of a different religion? Love them.

What about that Muslim family in my neighborhood? Love them.

What about people of a different sexual orientation? Love them.

What about immigrants? Love them.

What about the poor? Love them.

What about donkeys and elephants? Love them!

We do need to communicate the truth. But instead of "taking a stand for truth," communicate the truth about Jesus in the context of mercy made known by love. After all, Jesus said all people will know we are disciples not by shouting the truth and calling out people's failures, but rather by the way we love.

discussion **questions**

1. Outside of God, Jesus, and your family, what did you love the most as a child?

2. Describe what a person looks like when they have a lot of knowledge, but little love. How can we avoid being that kind of person?

3. Why is love confusing? Describe in your own words the different kinds of love you have experienced.

4. When you reflect upon the nature of God as a holy community of persons, what stands out to you the most?

5. What are the differences between rendering judgment from a place of anger and rendering judgment from a place of love?

6. What would it look like for you to prioritize other people in your world over yourself?

7. What person or group of people would you consider enemies? What can you do to actively love them?

8. With whom do you need to create an emotional boundary in order to resist codependency?

9. Is it easier for you to have mercy on yourself or others? Why?

10. What area of your life looks the least like love? What can you do to work on making it more loving?

6

Thinking

The Way of the Mind

"You need to get out of your mind and into your spirit," he said.

I heard these words as an impressionable young seminary student in my early twenties. I had been sitting behind my laptop in the small classroom listening to our guest lecturer for the day. He offered this unsolicited advice to me after class in an informal time of sharing. He was a Christian mystic of sorts, endeavoring not only to instruct, but to encourage as spontaneous thoughts would come to his mind. His presence didn't surprise me. I was at a Pentecostal/charismatic seminary after all. I assumed he took these spontaneous thoughts to be the Holy Spirit nudging him to share a word of encouragement. He spoke with a distinct accent, British or Australian, or a strange mixture of both. He was from out of town and was therefore an "expert" as far as I could tell, but his single-sentence message to me was strange. I was nearly halfway through seminary and the life of the mind was beginning to open to me in a new way. I had been a decent student in high school and college. My grades were acceptable, but I wasn't fully engaged. When I entered seminary after college graduation, I felt more engaged in what I was learning. My seminary professors didn't merely give me the right answers; they challenged me to work through complicated subjects and discover answers through thoughtful and prayerful exploration. My mind was being summoned to grow, my capacity to think was being expanded. But then I came upon this surprising roadblock.

This guest lecturer directly challenged me to abandon this mental enterprise in order to explore the world of the "spirit." The message was clear—if you are going to be a spiritual person, your mind will only get in the way. I scratched my head in response to his unexpected request. I quite literally shook my head as I wondered how I was supposed to "get out of my mind." In the end, I dismissed his instructions. Something didn't seem right. I certainly wanted to be a spiritual person in touch with a reality beyond the reach of my thoughts, but I couldn't conceive of a way to navigate myself into the world of the spirit without the use of my mind. His intentions were noble I suppose, but it's impossible to shut off one's mind in order to attune to one's spirit, because God made us integrated creatures.

THINKING CLEARLY AND CHRISTIANLY

I have found a way to live fully aware of the world of the spirit without leaving my mind behind. Sadly, many devout followers of Christ continue to buy into this false assumption that the life of the mind and the life of the spirit are somehow in conflict with each other. An alarming number of present-day followers of Christ resist, ignore, or simply don't understand the connectedness between the mind and spirit. They would rather feel their way through the faith and leave the thinking to somebody else. N. T. Wright observes, "Part of the problem in contemporary Christianity, I believe, is that talk about freedom of the Spirit, about the grace which sweeps us off our feet and heals and transforms our lives, has been taken over surreptitiously by a kind of low-grade romanticism, colluding with an anti-intellectual streak in our culture, generating the assumption that the more spiritual you are, the less you need to think."[1] Christians formed by a culture that would rather feel something spiritual than think about something conceptual have continued to resist the life of the mind. We are integrated beings; our heart and head are connected. Following Jesus in the way of the mind seeks to form a bridge between the mind and the spirit, the head and the heart, so that we grow in loving God with all our hearts *and* all our minds.

We need hearts ablaze with a desire for God and we need good thinking to guide the way. Wright continues, "Thinking clearly and Christianly is thus both a key element within the total rehumanizing process (you won't be fully human if you leave your thinking and reasoning behind) and a vital part of the motor which drives the rest of that process."[2] In awakening to the value of the Christian mind, we discover that all followers of Jesus are philosophers of a certain kind. Sadly there are not many philosophers among us. We don't find many people interested in anything philosophical because of the growing anti-intellectual sentiment around us. This vibe combined with the cultural pressure from bite-size pieces of information delivered rapid-fire via digital media has conditioned our minds in such a way that we struggle to think deeply or sustain the mental effort necessary to work through complex issues in our minds. My concern is not so much with the culture-wide absence of philosophical conversations, but how a lack of thinking has grown among Christians and kept so many followers of Christ underdeveloped.

It seems like many who call themselves evangelicals living in twenty-first-century America typically find little or no interest in philosophy, theology, or engaging the intellect. Mark Noll made this observation over twenty years ago when he declared, "The scandal of the evangelical mind is that there is not much of an evangelical mind."[3] While I see some signs of life in some pockets of evangelicalism (or post-evangelicalism), I continue to see far too many Christians languish in spiritual immaturity because they don't value their ability to think in relation to their faith. A steadily growing number of Christians hold the life of the mind in suspicion. Many followers of Jesus settle into surface-level conversations with one another, never daring to ask deep challenging questions about faith in Jesus, faith we hold so dear. As we consider the challenge to grow in how we think about God and God's world as followers of Jesus, let's answer some common questions.

Aren't we supposed to know God by encountering him and not just thinking about him? This question is often framed in the context of the difference between knowing God and knowing *about* God. Jesus, in his prayer in John 17, prayed, "Father, the hour has come; glorify your Son that the Son may glorify you, since you have given him authority over all flesh, to give eternal life to all whom you have given him. And this is eternal life, that they *know you* the only true God, and Jesus Christ whom you have sent" (John 17:1-3, emphasis mine). The experience of eternal life, according to Jesus, is to know God by direct personal encounter and not by piling up a mountain of "God-facts," a list of attributes describing what God is like.

Yet how are we to encounter him without some knowledge of him? And how are we supposed to have any knowledge of God without the use of our minds? Consider how normal human relationships work. Any encounter with another person includes communication—that is, the exchange of information through words, body language, tone of voice, etc. All of these expressions of communication are interpreted by our minds. I cannot have a direct personal encounter with people and really get to know them if I do not have the resources to interpret the words they use, or the reason they continue to roll their eyes when they talk about their boss. Our encounter with God is not dissimilar to our encounters with people. It includes communication, though the method is slightly different. We are not reading God's body language or trying to make sense of the tone in his voice, but we are listening, reading, worshiping, and interpreting in our minds what God is revealing about himself. We need to have our minds fully engaged when we encounter God. If we don't, then we can actually fail to connect with the God we are seeking. When we are "darkened in [our] understanding," we are "alienated from the life of God" (Ephesians 4:18). A true encounter with the living God is a matter of mind and spirit.

I'm not really "book smart"; shouldn't I just let other people do that thinking stuff for me? I'm aware of the arrogance of the intellectual community. Some high-level thinkers who spend their days in the halls of the academy's ivory tower or behind their computers pumping out books or blogs filled with complex, hard-to-understand words can certainly be intimidating. Knowledge has puffed them up, and they have not learned the Jesus way of love and humility. They can make you feel like any kind of good, reasonable, Christian thinking is out of reach, but you can't let other people get your thinking done for you. All of us can grow in the life of the mind, just like we can grow in any other area of life. We can all grow in how we think. We can all learn to think God's thoughts after him. We can learn to think new thoughts. We can learn to read books that today seem inaccessible. We can learn new words and increase our vocabulary. All of these things are possible, but like beginning to exercise for the first time, we have to start slowly and find a good plan for learning how to think well. Sure there will be professional Christian philosophers and theologians who will do a lot of the heavy academic thinking for us, but this does not mean we cannot grow in our ability to think through complex issues.

Aren't we supposed to be suspicious of philosophy and thinking too much? Often those who are fearful of walking down the road of reason and well-informed thinking quote verses like Colossians 2:8 to justify their suspicion of anything sounding like philosophy. At first reading, this verse sounds like a warning of the dangers of philosophy. Paul writes, "See to it that no one takes you captive by philosophy and empty deceit, according to human tradition, according to the elemental spirits of the world, and not according to Christ" (Colossians 2:8). But Paul isn't warning us about the dangers of philosophy per se; rather, he's warning us about a certain kind of philosophy. The word *philosophy* comes from two Greek words: *philo*, roughly translated "love," and *sophia*, meaning "wisdom." In its most basic form, philosophy is a love of wisdom. As Christians we do love a certain kind of wisdom, because for us wisdom is summed up in a person. Jesus is the one "who became to us wisdom from God" (1 Corinthians 1:30). If a philosopher is a lover of wisdom and if Jesus is the wisdom of God, then we are called to be philosophers of a certain kind. What makes us unique as lovers of wisdom is that we center our philosophy on Jesus Christ. We are to be skeptical of a philosophy based on mere human tradition, but we firmly embrace a philosophy based on Jesus Christ who is the wisdom of God in human form.

If we want to grow in our faith beyond simplistic religious platitudes, and if we want to be able to wrestle with the complex issues of our day, we need to learn to think clearly and Christianly. We find ourselves on unstable ground if we try to appropriate the Christian faith without Christian thinking. A healthy life in pursuit of Jesus is able to look at faith and explore the uncharted, mysterious dark corners of belief by asking questions, raising concerns, and yes, wrestling with doubt. Faithfulness to Jesus and the ways of Jesus doesn't mean we have it all figured out. Jesus gives us plenty of room to ask respectfully-framed questions about our faith as we continue to trust him. This description paints the picture of someone faithful to Christ. A religious fanatic dares not ask a single question. Religious fanaticism in general, and Christian fanaticism in particular, uncritically accepts any idea, teaching, or concept uttered by anyone claiming religious authority, without taking the time to verify whether or not the claim is in alignment with the Spirit of truth.

WHAT ARE YOU THINKING?

Good thinking as an intricate part of the Christian life comes to us in the form of a command from Jesus himself. When Jesus was asked to select the most important command from the entire Mosaic law recorded in the Old Testament, he responded by quoting the Jewish Shema from Deuteronomy. *Shema* is a Hebrew word meaning "hear" and it is the first word in this ancient and sacred prayer: "Hear, O Israel: The Lord our God, the Lord is one. You shall love the Lord your God with all your heart and with all your soul and with all your might" (Deuteronomy 6:4-5). Jesus quoted the Shema in answering the question about the most important commandment, but he added something. The Shema calls us to love God with three things, three areas of our being; Jesus adds a fourth. The Shema says to love God with heart, soul, and might. Jesus says love God with heart, soul, *mind*, and strength. All three references to the Shema in the Gospels (Matthew 22:37; Luke 10:27; and Mark 12:30) include the word *mind*. He also adds a second command to "love your neighbor as yourself" (Mark 12:31).

Jesus wants us to love God not only with our heart, soul, and might, but also with our mind, making us the kind of wisdom-lovers who center our thinking on the wisdom of God as revealed in Jesus. The earliest Christians of the first century carried out this call and command to love God with the mind, that is, with good thinking. We see this call to love with the mind carried on in the writings of the Paul who taught the church to think theologically and Christianly in his creation of what we know as Christian theology. Paul didn't give us a rulebook in his letters as much as he gave us the resources to think prayerfully in conversation with holy Scripture and the community of faith. The following is a brief sampling of how Jesus' command to love God with all of our minds was lived out in the life of the church.

"*For although they knew God, they did not honor him as God or give thanks to him, but they became futile in their thinking, and their foolish hearts were darkened*" (Romans 1:21). Those who ignore what can be seen of God in nature and in the cosmos are those who have become "futile in their thinking" because they cannot see the handiwork of God as they peer into the expanse of starry night, or stand at the foot of a mighty mountain, or lose themselves as the sun melts into the horizon of an expansive ocean. They did not rightly love God, because something was absent in their thinking.

"*For those who live according to the flesh set their minds on the things of the flesh, but those who live according to the Spirit set their minds on the things of the Spirit. For to set the mind on the flesh is death, but to set the mind on the Spirit is life and peace*" (Romans 8:5-6). Followers of Jesus are not given the option to choose thoughtful living over practical living. Rather, action and thinking go together; more specifically, thinking clearly and Christianly is one element in determining our behavior. We live out of our desires and we need them shaped by the Holy Spirit through ritual and Christian habits. But if we engage our thinking and intentionally set it on the things related to Jesus and the kingdom of God, then we will gravitate toward life and peace.

"*Do not be conformed to this world, but be transformed by the renewal of your mind, that by testing you may discern what is the will of God, what is good and acceptable and perfect. For by the grace given to me I say to everyone among you not to think of himself more highly than he ought to think, but to think with sober judgment, each according to the measure of faith that God has assigned"* (Romans 12:2-3). Followers of King Jesus in every age and in every village, town, and city around the world have faced the pressure to be conformed to the cultural values surrounding them. When Jesus prayed for his followers, he asked God not to take us out of the world, but to protect us from the evil one (John 17:15). The antidote to this cultural conformation is spiritual transformation, that is, the Holy Spirit doing its work to transform our minds.

"Brothers, do not be children in your thinking. Be infants in evil, but in your thinking be mature" (1 Corinthians 14:20). Paul offers this call to maturity while describing spiritual gifts and their use in public worship. Childish thinking about our life in the Spirit may be entertaining, but it will not produce the kind of church Jesus is building. We start as children in our thinking about God and we should find no shame in it. But we cannot remain children forever. We eventually need to grow up and take on some responsibility and begin to work on things requiring mature thoughts.

"But the wisdom from above is first pure, then peaceable, gentle, open to reason, full of mercy and good fruits, impartial and sincere" (James 3:17). Faulty wisdom produces jealousy, selfishness, and fighting. The kind of wisdom from above— that is, from God—is pure, peaceable, gentle, and reasonable. People who close themselves off to reason, and thus become unreasonable and thoughtless, turn down a road toward destruction. Dallas Willard describes those who are closed to reason as those plagued with "crooked thinking." He writes, "To serve God well we must think straight; and crooked think-ing, unintentional or not, always favors evil. And when the crooked thinking gets elevated into group orthodoxy, whether

religious or secular, there is always, quite literally, 'hell to pay.' That is, hell will take its portion, as it has repeatedly done in the horrors of world history."[4] An unreasonable life with its sham wisdom is both demonic and bent on destruction. These strong words serve as a bright, flashing neon sign warning us: if we want to experience the life of God, we need to remain open to reason so we can think straight.

THINKING ABOUT OUR THINKING

Jesus commanded us to love God with all of our minds, and the early Christian leaders encouraged the church to live out this commandment by living as a thinking community of people. Our sacred Scriptures bear witness to the inseparability of faith and reason. We cannot be faithful people without being reasonable people. We cannot be mature believers without being thinkers. We are more than thinking beings, but we are not less. So where do we begin in growing in our ability to love God with all our minds? We first need to do some thinking about thinking itself. *What is an idea? What is a thought? What is involved in the process of thinking?* I suppose there are numerous different ways to tackle these complex questions, but I would like to describe human thinking from the perspective of a pastor. I'm concerned first and foremost that as followers of Jesus we are thinking clearly and Christianly. As followers of Jesus we think clearly by slowing down, taking some time to think about our thinking. Here are some thoughts about our thinking.

Human thought is made up of ideas and images. At a very basic level our thinking is expressed in two distinct, but interrelated, mental expressions—ideas and images. Ideas are containers of information and images are pictures. Ideas are better explained in terms of abstract concepts, while images are best explained as specific pictures, often with an emotional connection. So for example, you have both the idea of a dog and an image of a dog in your mind. Your idea of a dog contains facts giving definition to what a dog is: a four-legged domesticated mammal with fur, panting, barking, etc. You also have a picture of a dog in your mind. Perhaps it is an iconic dog from pop culture like Lassie, Rin Tin Tin, Old Yeller, Toto, or Benji. Perhaps it is the image of a dog you had as a pet when you were a child. This image is a snapshot of a specific dog. These work together, informing one another and shaping one another, as we think about a dog. As we grow in our ability to think well, we ask ourselves: *What do we do with all these ideas and images? How do we put them together in a helpful way? How do we order them in such a way that we are led to truth? How do we evaluate our ideas and images? Which ones need to change? What new ideas do we need to add? What old images do we need to purge from our thinking?* Questions like these lead us to the next description of human thought.

Thinking is a kind of internal monologue. We have all had those little conversations with ourselves within our own heads. Sometimes we vocalize them and begin talking to ourselves, which can get a little weird. Talking out loud when we are the only audience can be a bit strange, but talking to ourselves inwardly is a helpful way to understand what thinking is all about. This internal monologue is one of the ways we talk things out within ourselves. Maybe we jot things down on a piece of paper to get the thoughts out and in front of us so we can continue the conversation in our heads. We know we are created in God's triune image. Perhaps when we talk to ourselves without spoken words, we are reflecting the image of God. Often we conduct this mental conversation when we need to make a decision. We tell people, "I just need time to think." So we find time to sit down and begin a conversation in our heads. We replay ideas and images. We try to make connections between certain ideas and images. We weigh the strengths of the pros and cons. We try to form a conclusion or decision and we do this by thinking.

Thinking is a kind of reflection. Whenever we review past information, we draw up memories and begin to rewind the tape on events and experiences we have lived through. We re-examine thoughts from the past, perhaps unfiled thoughts that we have shelved in our memory banks. Maybe we reminisce, replaying in our heads stories from our past. We call these stored up ideas and images memories. Our memories inform how we think about the present. For example, systemic, widespread, cultural racism is the product of present thinking based on painful experiences and memories from the past. Whether it is racism experienced between Palestinians and Israelis in the Middle East or Indians and Pakistanis in Asia or blacks and whites in the United States, years of injustice and mistrust have shaped present thinking so that it's difficult for one group to extend hands of genuine friendship to those on the other side. This kind of harmful reflection needs an injection of new experience and thinking in order to heal the memories of the past.

Thinking requires mental energy and effort. Thinking isn't like getting up every day and working with a sledgehammer, but it's hard work nonetheless. It doesn't require physical strength, although a case can be made that physical health affects our capacity to think well. Thinking isn't physical work, but it does require a great deal of energy and effort—mental work can drain us of energy just as much as physical work. Honestly, the amount of mental energy necessary in human thinking is why some Christians struggle to think well. I offer this observation not as a judgment but as a description of the tremendous amount of work that goes into thinking well. We all think, but the question to ask is whether or not we are thinking *well. Are we thinking clearly? Are we thinking in a way that takes into consideration all the scraps of knowledge on a certain subject? Are we thinking in a way that aligns our thinking with the mind of Jesus?* Thinking well requires us to pay attention with a sharp mental focus, to eliminate distractions and think about one subject for a prolonged amount of time. Thinking well includes a kind of mental combat. We battle to "take every thought captive to obey Christ" (2 Corinthians 10:5). None of these aspects of our thought life is easy. None of them can be accomplished without a commitment to spend the necessary mental energy to do the work.

Thinking is how we process information. We are hard-wired to observe. We learn, whether in a classroom or not. We see. We hear. We read. We listen. We study. We feel. We take in information and store it in an idea, or we take a mental picture and store it in our memory banks. We begin to think when we start to do something with these ideas and images. We identify them. We put them in little compartments in our minds with similar ideas or images. We make connections. We begin to test the validity of each idea. We evaluate. We render judgment, calling some ideas true and some ideas false, or we simply set them off to the side on an out-of-the-way shelf in our minds to figure out when more information comes. We do this more often than we realize. For example, when we go to a new restaurant for the first time, the first thing we are handed when we sit down is a menu. When we begin to look over the menu we look at the meal options. We look at the prices. We read the detailed description of what goes into each entree. We look at the pictures and wonder if the actual food will look that good. We ask questions of those we are eating with or get recommendations from the server. All of these simple tasks are acts of observation and data gathering. Our thinking kicks in when we begin to categorize this new information with what we already know about other foods we have eaten. Then we begin to evaluate our options. *Do I want beef or chicken? Maybe I should eat vegetarian? Wow, the steak meal is only twelve dollars; that sounds like a good deal! What is a balsamic glaze? Should I really spend that much for salmon? My friend recommends the pork, but the server says the grilled chicken is the best. How many calories are in that pasta plate?* We evaluate our meal options based on past experiences and values such as diet, nutrition, and cost. When we evaluate like this we are engaged in the process of thinking, whether we realize it or not.

Thinking is a way we connect the dots. Very similar to this observation and evaluation is the process of connecting two or more ideas or images together. Just like observation and evaluation, we also do this all the time. Let's say you walk into your kitchen before suppertime and you see a pack of Oreos opened upon the counter. You can see the packaging has been torn a little and some cookies are missing. Then you walk into little Mary's bedroom and you see black crumbs all over her face. It does not take you very long to connect these two ideas. Someone opened the Oreos and Mary has black Oreo crumbs on her face. I see the connection—Mary got into the cookies!

Sometimes we falsely connect dots because we do not have all the information. Maybe someone else opened the cookies and gave one to Mary. At other times we connect the *wrong dots* and form wrong conclusions. These are called logical fallacies, because we are falsely using logic. For example, I can make the following statements. Sadly, the first two are true, but the conclusion is faulty.

Statement 1: The Kansas City Royals are bad.

Statement 2: The Kansas City Royals are a baseball team.

Conclusion: Baseball teams are bad.

In formal logic this is an example of an association fallacy. The first statement is true. The Royals won the 2015 World Series and since then—nothing! It is also true to say the Royals are a baseball team. However, the conclusion is false, because the wrong dots were connected. In connecting "bad" and "baseball team," I made a faulty conclusion by not thinking clearly about baseball (or the Royals).

Thinking is a kind of worldview. A "worldview" is quite simply how we view the world around us. Once we connect enough dots forming a web of ideas, we form a worldview, which becomes a lens by which we interpret life, people, and ideas all around us. This worldview forms a distinct point of view or an internal bias that guides how we understand things and make decisions. We do not download a worldview in a matter of seconds, but we develop a worldview over time as we connect dots. If we never learn to think well and we connect the wrong dots or connect dots in a wrong order, then our worldview will be misshapen. In other words, bad thinking leads to a bad worldview.

Consider the previous example of bad thinking regarding the Kansas City Royals. Suppose this kind of bad thinking is applied to people and not just a baseball team. What if our thinking was something like this:

Statement 1: Tom is poor.

Statement 2: Tom is lazy.

Conclusion: The poor are lazy.

These statements represent the same kind of poor thinking we encountered in the example about baseball, but this thinking begins to shape our worldview regarding the poor. If we are following Jesus, then we must admit that our views on baseball are far less important than our views of the poor. I don't believe Jesus is interested in sports as much as he is interested in the poor and oppressed. If we want a Christ-informed worldview, we need to learn to think well. So if we begin to connect the right kind of dots we can make statements like this:

Statement 1: The poor are people.

Statement 2: People are created in the image of God with worth and dignity.

Conclusion: The poor are created with worth and dignity.

In this example, we are connecting the dots in the right and more helpful order: poor—people—dignity. This kind of good thinking produces a good worldview, one much more in line with the values of Christ.

If we are going to think well and love God with all of our mind, we start by reflecting on our thinking. In other words, we can begin to develop our capacity to think once we have some understanding of what it means to think clearly. In following Jesus we want to think not only clearly, but also Christianly. We want to renew our minds so that we might think God's thoughts after him. We want minds conformed to the image and mind of Jesus. We want to connect the dots between God, people, creation, and human responsibility like Jesus did. Developing minds like Jesus requires more than good thinking. We also need to give the Holy Spirit freedom to do the good work of transformation.

discussion **questions**

1. What were some of the silly things you would say or do as a child? If you have children, what are some of the silly things they say?

2. Do you feel more connected to the thoughts in your head or the feelings in your heart? Or both? Explain.

3. What does it mean to think both clearly and Christianly?

4. Does the challenge to grow in the life of the mind intimidate you? Why or why not?

5. How have you experienced the renewing of your mind? For example, what established cultural norms did you once hold but have rethought since following Jesus?

6. How would you describe someone with mature thinking?

7. Do you think out loud? Write things down? Talk to yourself? What does thinking as reflection look like for you?

8. How would you describe your thinking? Do you compartmentalize your thoughts? Do you think more in ideas or images?

9. What do you do when your thinking is unclear and fuzzy?

10. How can you grow in thinking thoughts like Jesus?

7

Change

The Way of Transformation

When Jesus invites us to come to him, his invitation requires nothing more than our willingness to follow him. Accepting this invitation implies we trust Jesus and are willing to rethink everything in the light of him. Jesus doesn't want us to hide from him, ashamed of our past. Jesus sees us and accepts us as we are, faults and all. He doesn't love us simply because he sees potential in us. He doesn't love us for what we can do for God and others. He doesn't love us in order to get something from us. Jesus loves us because he is the full embodiment of perfect love. He loves us with full knowledge of our weaknesses and imperfections. He invites us to come just as we are, but he doesn't expect us to remain as we are. We accept God's love for us and we begin to follow Jesus and then we slowly start looking more like Jesus. *At least, we are supposed to look like Jesus.* Unfortunately, all of the research that has been done over the last decade reveals that those who claim to be Christians are, by and large, not very Christlike.

In a recent research project, the Barna Group determined that 51 percent of self-identifying Christians tended to have attitudes and actions that are characterized by self-righteousness. Only 14 percent of self-identified Christians represented actions and attitudes consistent with those of Jesus.[1] The results of this research can be a bit of a shock, but unfortunately if anyone spends any time around the church, it doesn't take long to see this report is true. The labels "self-righteous" or "hypocritical" have become the common reputation of Christians held by those outside the church. While large numbers of non-Christian people have a positive impression of Jesus, many of these same people have negative feelings about the people who claim to be following Jesus. Scandals in church leadership in both Roman Catholic churches and evangelical megachurches have amplified this negative reputation. We are supposed to be a reflection of Jesus, but without a clear path of discipleship we tend to reflect the assumed values of the culture around us. We are supposed to be a living reminder of Jesus, but sadly we are too often a living reminder of the brokenness of our world. The solution is to take a radical turn and rediscover our roots, in order to ground ourselves in the ancient practices of Christians who have been following Jesus for centuries. We need to be honest about our moral failures and character deficiencies and be willing to change.

BEING TRANSFORMED

Change for followers of Jesus looks like whole-life transformation. As we experience change we find ourselves in a process of metamorphosis much like what a caterpillar experiences as it becomes a butterfly. As Paul writes, "Now the Lord is the Spirit, and where the Spirit of the Lord is, there is freedom. And we all, with unveiled face, beholding the glory of the Lord, are being transformed into the same image from one degree of glory to another. For this comes from the Lord who is the Spirit" (2 Corinthians 3:17-18). We do not change ourselves, but we are the recipients of change. Learning new skills and habits certainly has its place in Christian discipleship. As followers of Jesus we adopt practices that reflect the life of Jesus. We can do things that improve our lives and cause us to grow and mature, but the deep-level change of our hearts and minds is the work of the Lord who is the Spirit. We call this process "spiritual transformation," not specifically because it's our spiritual selves that are being transformed, even though transformation includes the formation of our hearts into Christlikeness. Rather, this transformation is spiritual because it's a process driven and directed by the Holy Spirit.

Spiritual transformation is the spirituality of discipleship, which becomes the engine that powers the kind of lives we live patterned after the life of Jesus. The Holy Spirit coordinates a change inside us that matches the change in lifestyle that can be seen on the outside. Trying to change our behavior without also allowing for heart change leads us in the way of hypocritical religion, the way of the Pharisees. Jesus reserved his harshest critique for this group. The Pharisees were a group of Jewish people who were strict followers of the commands of the Old Testament and many other traditions. They assumed that if they could live perfectly according to God's law, God's kingdom would come. Jesus called them hypocrites, that is, pretenders or play actors. They focused on smaller things like going through their spice rack and figuring out exactly how much of each spice to give to God, while all along neglecting the "weightier matters" of the Jewish law, things like "justice and mercy and faithfulness" (Matthew 23:23). Worse yet, they emphasized outward behavior and practices and neglected character formation, the work of the heart.

Jesus called the Pharisees "whitewashed tombs," because their lives looked all right on the outside, but on the inside they were full of dead people's bones (Matthew 23:27). They tied their devotion to God to how they looked in public. Their lack of dedication to the formation of their souls left their character decimated; their paper-thin shell of outward devotion ultimately cracked under pressure. A human life isn't designed to withstand the pressures of life with hearts empty, dark, and cold. In following Jesus we want to be people who walk in the ways of justice and mercy because we have hearts formed in justice and mercy. Trying really hard to look like we are followers of Jesus without the slow methodical process of real heart change is the road to hypocrisy. In the way of transformation, we choose to give up on trying to be Christian. Willpower manifested in clenched teeth and a white-knuckled grip will only go so far. In this way the invitation to follow Jesus is an invitation to quit trying to follow Jesus in our own strength, quit leaning on our own understanding, quit trusting in our own abilities. First quit, and then open up to the Spirit's work. As we do so we find the character formation to match the way we live.

We need a renewed vision of spiritual transformation rooted in the historic Christian tradition and the Trinity. As noted in chapter 5, language of the Trinity is how Christians talk about God. The God revealed in Jesus and experienced by the Holy

Spirit is the God of Israel, the one God of creation, the one true and living God who has been revealed as Father, Son, and Holy Spirit. As we have seen, the most fundamental discovery in our understanding of the Trinity is that God is love. This very divine love has been "poured into our hearts through the Holy Spirit who has been given to us" (Romans 5:5). We love God and others by the love God gives us through the Holy Spirit. In this way we are empowered by the Spirit to become people of love and people who love. God gives us this power to shape us and form us on the inside so we can be whole and then express that love to others. Our understanding of spiritual transformation is shaped by our understanding of the Trinity. Spiritual transformation is the work of the Holy Spirit to transform us into the image of Jesus for the joy of God the Father. The Spirit does this work in the context of Christian community as we walk along spiritual pathways. Let's consider each part of this definition.

THE WORK OF THE SPIRIT

The besetting sin of our secular age is the sin of self-sufficiency. With God obscured from view, modern secular people are left with little more than human-generated attempts to change society and perhaps to change themselves. God has been kicked off his throne and "enlightened" humanity has elevated the autonomous thinking self to the ultimate place of power and control. Any talk of spirituality gets reduced to the power of the human spirit. Followers of Jesus who drink deeply from this well pay lip service to the God of Christian worship, and work at change fueled by willpower. We should certainly put forth effort in following Jesus, but it's not human-generated hard work where our sole dependence is on the energy we can muster up. Jesus offers us a better way forward. The way of transformation is not a matter of willpower, but a willingness to be open to the Spirit's power.

Jesus said he would not leave us to human effort alone. He told us, "If you love me, you will keep my commandments" (John 14:15). Nothing surprising here. All religious leaders give their followers commands to carry out. What makes Jesus unique is that he gives both commands and the power to obey those commands. Jesus continued by saying, "And I will ask the Father, and he will give you another Helper, to be with you forever, even the Spirit of truth, whom the world cannot receive, because it neither sees him nor knows him. You know him, for he dwells with you and will be in you" (John 14:16-17). As John the Baptist said, he would baptize with water, but Jesus would come to baptize us in the Holy Spirit. As we are immersed in the Spirit of truth, we have been promised power, not just power to *do*, but power to *be*, power to become living reflections of Jesus himself.

The Holy Spirit is like a master sculptor with hammer and chisel in hand, chipping away everything from our lives that doesn't look like Jesus. A part of this chipping away is the Spirit's work of reorienting our desires for the things of God. The Spirit doesn't extinguish our desires but redirects them toward love, joy, peace, and all of the fruit of the Spirit. This work changes the look of our interior life so we can become our true selves, the people God has created us to be. We can choose to work with the Holy Spirit in becoming more like Jesus or we can work against it. When we practice things like awareness, learning, reflection, and action we work with the Spirit who is the presence of God, our teacher in the school of King Jesus, our guide in the process of reflection, and the energy behind all our action. As we cultivate an ongoing relationship with the Holy Spirit we can begin to detect the Spirit's prompting, leading us to Jesus.

THE IMAGE OF JESUS

If the Spirit is the artist, then Jesus is the model. Jesus is our Lord and he is God's Son, very "God from God, Light from Light, true God from true God, begotten, not made, of one Being with the Father" as we confess in the words of the Nicene Creed. Jesus is the second person of the Trinity, distinct from the Father, but fully God. Jesus is also fully human, the prototype of what we are to become. If we want to know what God is like we look at Jesus. If we want to know what humanity is supposed to be like, we look at Jesus. The Spirit molds and shapes us, so that we become honest reflections of the life of Jesus. Thomas à Kempis opens his classic work *The Imitation of Christ* with these words, "'Anyone who follows me shall not walk in darkness,' says the Lord. These are the words of Christ, and by them we are reminded that we must imitate his life and his ways if we are to be truly enlightened and set free from the darkness of our own hearts. Let it be the most important thing we do, then, to reflect on the life of Jesus Christ."[2]

The great promise that "all things work together for good" is given to those who are "called according to God's purpose" (Romans 8:28). A lot of attention is given to this verse, and for good reason. This little promise tucked away in Paul's massively complex letter to the church in Rome has been the source of encouragement for followers of Jesus suffering through moments of difficulty and loss. But what exactly is God's purpose? In one sense our purpose is to love God, to enjoy God, to live in obedience to God. All of these answers are true insofar as they correspond to the purpose given to us in the very next verse, "For those whom he foreknew he also predestined *to be conformed to the image of his Son*, in order that he might be the firstborn among many brothers" (Romans 8:29, emphasis mine). Jesus is God's Son and we are all sons and daughters of God who look up to Jesus as our big brother. While God does not cause all things, we can trust God will cause all things to work together for good for those who willingly participate in God's plan to form us into the image of Jesus.

Dallas Willard developed a model of spiritual transformation using the acronym VIM—vision, intent, and means.[3] It begins with vision—that is, what we see. We need an adequate vision of our transformation. *What will we look like when we are transformed? What does a fully transformed person look like? What is the enfleshed goal we are striving toward?* The answer is Jesus. The Spirit enlivens our intent and redirects our desires, so that we are serious about our intentions. The church gives us the means, which are ancient spiritual pathways. God offers Jesus as the vision of our transformation. The beautiful life, death, and resurrection of Jesus shines bright as the glowing prototype of a human being fully alive. As we remain persistent in following Jesus with Spirit-empowered intent, we will find a never-ending journey of fascination. With our eyes full of Jesus, fixed unwaveringly to the ways of Jesus, we will become like him. It's human nature to become like those upon whom we fix our attention. Jesus provides the vision. Illuminated and endued with power from the Spirit, we provide the intent. The church provides the means so that we may walk in the footsteps of Jesus.

To walk in this way, the way of transformation, means we are being changed to ultimately act like Jesus. This truth doesn't mean we will become robotic clones. The more we are being transformed to look and act like Jesus, the more we find ourselves distinguished from other followers of Jesus. Becoming like Jesus doesn't diminish our uniqueness. Some of us will choose to eat meat, and some of us will not. Some of us will choose to drink alcohol in moderation, some of us will not. Some of us will listen to popular music, some of us will not. Some of us will choose to homeschool our children, some of us will not. Some of us will be Christlike introverts. Some of us will be Christlike extroverts. Some of us will be Christlike artists. Some of us will be Christlike accountants. The beauty in the Holy Spirit's work in changing us to reflect the action of Jesus is the diversity. We discover over time that as we are becoming more like Jesus, we are becoming our true selves, unique expressions of the image of Jesus. As we are all being changed to act like Jesus, the Holy Spirit will lead us in different ways, always in love, but in ways that draw out our distinctiveness. We should enjoy and celebrate the richness of our diversity as followers of Jesus.

THE JOY OF GOD THE FATHER

We are ultimately being transformed for the joy of God the Father, and not only for our own benefit. We certainly reap the rewards in becoming more like Jesus. We find our true selves. We become the kind of people God has designed us to be. In this way we are fully alive, fully human, and fully confident we are loved. As the psalmist writes, "Bless the Lord, O my soul, and all that is within me, bless his holy name! Bless the Lord, O my soul, and forget not all his benefits" (Psalm 103:1-2).

Perhaps nothing is more satisfying and more beneficial than the self-awareness of knowing who I am and where I am supposed to be. But placing God's joy over our own sense of satisfaction guards against turning spiritual transformation into some kind of cheap version of Christianized self-help. Eugene Peterson's translation of Jesus in Matthew 16 is helpful here: "Anyone who intends to come with me has to let me lead. You're not in the driver's seat; *I* am. Don't run from suffering; embrace it. Follow me and I'll show you how. Self-help is no help at all. Self-sacrifice is the way, my way, to finding yourself, your true self. What kind of deal is it to get everything you want but lose yourself? What could you ever trade your soul for?" (Matthew 16:24-26 *The Message*). We find our true selves by prioritizing God's joy over our own.

The joy experienced by God the Father is the overflow of the love expressed between the Father, Son, and Holy Spirit. Tagging close behind the self-giving love within the members of the Trinity is an authentic and abiding joy. What becomes predominant in the story of Jesus is how much God the Father loves Jesus with a love that is dripping with joy. God loves his Son just like any father does. I understand how God feels in this regard because I have three sons—Wesley, Taylor, and Dylan. I love them and I'm so proud of them not because of what they do, even though I cannot hide the feelings of pride that well up in my heart when they accomplish great things. My love for them is based in who they are. God made each of my boys different and unique, but each one of them is kind, considerate, thoughtful. They are young men of integrity and character. I cannot help but to be proud! With the mistakes I've made as a father I consider it a gift from God. Though I don't express it enough, the love I feel for my sons is an expression of God's work in my heart and theirs. Never was God the Father's love for the Son on display in clearer terms in the Gospels than at the baptism of Jesus.

John the Baptist was baptizing people in the Jordan River when Jesus approached. We shouldn't be surprised this entire episode took place at the Jordan. This river is where the people of God crossed from the wilderness and into God's Promised Land. Jesus had come to lead the entire world into God's new world of forgiveness, healing, and peace, and so he had to reenact a crossing of the Jordan River. When John saw Jesus drawing near he exclaimed, "Behold, the Lamb of God, who takes away the sin of the world!" (John 1:29). John resisted for a moment, explaining that Jesus should be the one doing the baptizing, but Jesus was insistent. He told John, "Let it be so now, for thus it is fitting for us to fulfill all righteousness" (Matthew 3:15). The time was right for Jesus to pass through the waters of the Jordan, because this was the right time to carry forth God's covenant plan to rescue the world through the people of Abraham, the people who gave birth to Jesus who would become King.

John consented and then lowered Jesus into the fresh, steadily moving water. When Jesus emerged from the water he took his first breath in God's new mission for him. Then the most surprising thing happened. In the events that happened next we see the Trinity on display. The heavens opened up and God the Holy Spirit descended like a dove and rested on the shoulder of God the Son. Then a voice thundered from heaven saying, "This is my beloved Son, with whom I am well pleased" (Matthew 3:17). In other words, when God the Father saw his Son coming up out of the water, he knew Jesus was beginning his mission of announcing and inaugurating the kingdom of God. Like a soccer mom whose son just kicked the winning goal, God leapt from his throne in heaven and with a heart bursting with joy proclaimed, "This is my Son, the one I love. He makes me so happy!" I understand the joy of this moment. I have had the privilege of baptizing all three of my boys. I can recall the excited feeling as each one confessed faith in Jesus and affirmed his commitment to follow Jesus all the days of his life. I was so happy at the baptism of my sons. God was overwhelmingly happy at the baptism of his. Because God the Father and God the Son are bound together with love and joy, God the Father is overjoyed every time he sees his Son. So as God the Father looks over the rail of heaven and sees the image of his Son being formed in our hearts, God again exclaims, "There is the Son I love and he makes me happy!"

THE CONTEXT OF CHRISTIAN COMMUNITY

When the original followers of Jesus received the Holy Spirit on the day of Pentecost, Peter stood up to address the crowd and he quoted from Joel 2, saying, "And in the last days it shall be, God declares, that I will pour out my Spirit on all flesh" (Acts 2:17). God made the Spirit available to all people in all cultures without exclusion. God is everywhere present on the earth by the Holy Spirit. To claim that Christians somehow have the Holy Spirit locked away in a church closet is ridiculous. As we follow the empowering work of the Spirit throughout the emerging story of the church in the book of Acts and throughout the rest of the Bible, we see that the epicenter of the Spirit's eruptions is located in the middle of the gathering of God's people. In other words, the work of the Spirit in all that the Spirit does is not isolated to individuals. The Spirit works in the context of Christian community. The building up of the local gathering of followers of Jesus—what we call the church—is what Jesus is doing, and this is the place where the empowerment and encouragement of the Spirit can be found. We gather together on Sundays to worship, celebrate, encourage one another, proclaim the gospel, and to be formed by the Spirit in the ways of Jesus.

Merely attending a church gathering doesn't change us, but it does put us in a place where we can be changed. We will explore this idea in more depth in the next chapter, but suffice it to say that we cannot be fully formed in the image of Jesus without regular participation in the life of the local church. When I hear people speak in glowing terms about Jesus and then trash the church, I pause for a moment. I'm surprised people can callously call the church worthless, pointless, and filled with hypocrisy, because the church is the bride of Jesus after all! I learned from an early age that I may be able to challenge a grown man, but I better not dare start talking trash about his bride! If we love Jesus and we are following Jesus, then we need to love what Jesus loves. When Paul tells husbands to love their wives, he tells them to do so "as Christ loved the church and gave himself up for her" (Ephesians 5:25). Jesus loved the church, the gathering of his followers, and gave himself for us. The church is imperfect because it is comprised of imperfect people. Regardless of our sincerity in following Jesus, we will always love one another imperfectly. Jesus knows our struggles to live out what we believe is true, but he never said he was done with the church. He actually said the opposite! He told us he would be with us always, even "to the end of the age" (Matthew 28:20).

When we engage in Christian community, we repent of the sin of self-sufficiency. When we joyfully (and sometimes reluctantly) commit ourselves to be participants in the local church, we find ourselves worshiping, praying, sharing meals, and serving side by side with all sorts of people. The Spirit uses the people we worship with to form us into the image of Jesus. Finding friends at church is irreplaceable if we are going to follow Jesus faithfully, because of the irrefutable principle of association, which states that we will become like the people with whom we invest quality time. I first discovered this principle when I served as a youth pastor. Youth culture is dominated by cliques. All you have to do is walk into a high school lunch room and there you will find them: the cool kids, the rich kids, the jocks, the band geeks, the stoners, and the freaks. Everyone wants to be an individual, but everyone in that lunch room is shaped by their tribe. This principle isn't only a youth phenomenon. It extends into adulthood and it works its way into church life.

If we want to remain faithful to the ways of Jesus, then we need to spend time with people who want to remain faithful, which is why church is so important. Friends provide a framework in which the Spirit is at work forming us to look like Jesus. But participation in the life of the local church is not only hanging out with our friends. The church Jesus is building is multicultural. The beauty of Christian community is that we not only gather together with our friends, but we also gather with people we would not necessarily choose to spend time with otherwise. Learning to love those who are not like us is integral to becoming more like Jesus.

SPIRITUAL PATHWAYS

The Spirit transforms us as we gather in Christian community. This facet of the way of transformation is made known in what we do with others. The Spirit also transforms us as we walk along spiritual pathways. These paths are the practices we do on our own. We need both. In this way, following Jesus is neither all public nor all private. Following Jesus isn't only what we do with other people. We need to walk in Christian community and we need to walk down spiritual pathways if we want to flourish as followers of Jesus. This truth will challenge both introverts who draw their strength and renew their energy in isolation and extroverts who become energized being with other people. Spiritual pathways invite us to go down well-worn trails walked by countless brothers and sisters in Christ who have gone before us. These pathways are habits like prayer, Scripture, contemplation, silence, solitude, fasting, and worship.

These pathways aren't new trails we're blazing. The saints of old have carved these trails into the rocky earth. The way of Jesus is an ancient way. While we may find new discoveries on the way and while we may interpret the ways of Jesus in a way that makes sense to the time and culture in which we live, we don't create the ways of Jesus. They have been given to us. They have been passed down to us from generations and generations of Christians going back nearly two thousand years. Every local church has its own specific traditions and these practices may differ from church to church, but we have been given a great tradition, a grand collection of spiritual pathways that we are all invited to explore. We should hold fast to these traditions as we have been so encouraged, "So then, brothers, stand firm and hold to the traditions that you were taught by us, either by our spoken word or by our letter" (2 Thessalonians 2:15). We hold fast to these spiritual pathways not to elevate them above the commands of Jesus, but because as we walk down them, we find ourselves in places where we can grow in the grace that empowers us to obey those commands.

We will explore these pathways in more detail in chapter 9, but they begin and end with prayer, the root of all spiritual pathways. Just like community, prayer does not change us, but prayer puts us in a place where we can be changed. Prayer carves out moments in our day to make space for God. Prayer causes us to grow in our awareness of God. We need to learn to pray with the saints of old. We need prayer books and liturgies. We need to memorize prayers that prevent us from turning prayer into a nonstop plea for God to give us what we want. We should certainly make our requests known to God and pour out our hearts to God, but as we will discover, prayer is so much more than that.

Prayer, like all spiritual pathways, is a matter of training, because what you can't do by *trying* you can do by *training*. As John Ortberg points out, "[Training] means to arrange your life around certain exercises and experiences that will enable you to do eventually what you are not yet able to do even by trying hard."[4] Think about weight lifting. I haven't lifted weights since I was in high school, but imagine what it would look like if I tried to bench press three hundred pounds. I could find one of those guys in the gym with bulging muscles to spot me. I could have the music cranked up in the gym. I could get my new muscle-bound friend to give me a pep talk in a voice that sounds like a cross between a Pentecostal preacher and a pro wrestler. I could lay down on the bench and have my friend help me lift the bar loaded down with weights. I could lower the bar to my chest and try to push that bar up into the air. I could try *really hard*. I could grunt and shout from my increasingly red face, and do you know what would happen? Nothing. That bar would sit on my chest because either I can bench press three hundred pounds or I can't; trying has nothing to do with it! The way of transformation is the Spirit's work, forming us into the image of Jesus for the joy of God the Father. We work with the Spirit not by trying but by training. So feel free to quit. If you have tried to follow Jesus and have failed because it doesn't seem to work for you then just quit. Don't quit on Jesus, but quit trying. Give up on doing things your own way and quit trying to do things in your own strength. The way of Jesus is ready-made for quitters. So quit on willpower and come join us as we train in the ways of Jesus together.

discussion **questions**

1. What is the hardest lifestyle change you have had to make in your life? Perhaps it is related to diet, exercise, spending habits . . . or is it something else?

2. Why do so many people seek to make outward changes in behavior before experiencing the inward changes of character?

3. Does an openness to God's Spirit encourage you, or cause you to pause cautiously?

4. Considering the perfection of Jesus, do you feel intimidated or encouraged in trying to pattern your life after his?

5. What brings you the most joy in life?

6. How do your friends who are following Jesus encourage you in your pursuit of King Jesus?

7. How does loving people who are not like you make you more like Jesus?

8. What spiritual pathways have you found to be the most helpful for you?

9. What are the key differences between *trying* to be Christian and *training* to be Christian?

10. What do you need to quit trying to do in pursuit of Jesus?

8

Gathering
The Way of Community

I 'm not religious; I just love the Lord."

This black-and-white bumper sticker was proudly displayed on my 1978 Mustang II when I was a teenager in the early 1990s. My faith had taken an enormous step forward just months before I obtained a license from the state of Missouri to legally operate a motor vehicle. My first car was one of the ugly Mustangs, but nevertheless I was eager to display my faith in the very clichéd form of a bumper sticker, so the world would know my faith wasn't a half-hearted attempt to win over the affections of my parents. My faith was real and I wasn't just being religious. My bumper-sticker-faith-confession plastered on the exterior of my car was my way of communicating what was on the inside of me. I'd encountered Jesus not as an idea, not as a religious leader, but as the living

Christ. His love had overwhelmed me and seemingly overnight transformed me. So I intended to pursue him in order to know him, to worship him, and yes, to love him. Jesus, whom my bumper sticker called "the Lord," had captured my attention. Religion? Not so much. I wasn't interested in religion in the ways my naive mind understood religion at the time: a lifeless, stuffy, traditional, ritualistic form of worship that lacked intentionality and energy.

In those early days of following Jesus, religion seemed utterly uncompelling. Thoughts of religion brought to my mind pictures of churches asleep in the light. I wanted nothing to do with sleepy-eyed congregations walking through dead rituals and reciting monotone litanies, where faith was not alive and active, where attention to rules and rituals eclipsed following Jesus with reckless abandonment. As a sixteen-year-old with a heart bursting with the love of God, I wanted to walk in the footsteps of Jesus. Religion for me at that time was simply another word for church. The church only interested me when they talked about Jesus. I went to church and participated in the weekly activities of the church because I wanted to know more about Jesus. The church itself was secondary. I even took the time to write the word *religion* with a line drawn through it in the margin of a page in my Bible. I was willing to tolerate the church and its "religion" as it supplied me what I needed to know about Jesus, but I didn't want to be known as one of those prudish, demure, church-going religious types. I wanted to follow Jesus and that was all. Little did I know that the only reason I knew about Jesus was that the church had in fact been practicing the Christian religion for nearly two millennia. My juvenile disdain for the church did not last very long.

Not two months after I slapped that bumper sticker on my car, I knew I would serve the church for the rest of my life. It was a Monday in August before the beginning of my junior year in high school. I had attended a Bible study that night where our youth pastor talked about the difference between *agape* love and *philo* love. God loves us, I was told, with *agape* love, with an unending, unconditional love. This kind of love was stronger than *philo*, a love marked by brotherly affection. I went home after that Bible study with the thoughts of *agape* love swimming in mind. I thought, "If God loves me with a never-dying love then maybe I should love him with that same kind of love." This reflection accompanied me as I tried to go to sleep but I couldn't bring to shore the thoughts that had set sail in my head. I was asking myself, "Do I love God? Do I really love God? Do I love him the way he loves me?" I knew I did, but I had never uttered it aloud. I pulled back the covers and sat up in the darkness of my bedroom. I put my feet on the floor and began to pray.

I don't remember every word of that prayer, but I do remember saying one thing: "God, I love you with an *agape* kind of love. I love you more than anything." As soon as I prayed these words it felt like I lost all the strength in my body. I slumped down on my knees with my head on the floor. I didn't adopt this posture of prayer because I had been trained to do so. I had had little exposure to the charismatic renewal. I'd never been to a Pentecostal church. I wasn't mimicking anything I had seen. I was experiencing something genuine, something transcendent, something of the work of the Holy Spirit. In that moment I was keenly aware of God's presence and a thought entered my mind in a brilliant flash that almost sounded like a voice. This voice in my head said, "Ministry."

I replied, "God if you are calling me into full-time ministry, then I say yes!" This special encounter with the Holy Spirit was dramatic. We should expect to have experiences with God, because God isn't a subject that we study as much as a person we can encounter. We should always be open to the surprising work of God, but experiences like these are rare. When they come we should treasure them, because they have the power to change us. That night something changed in me. My love for Jesus expanded into my love for the people of God whom Jesus asked me to serve for the rest of my life.

I shouldn't have had such a negative attitude about the church, because the church had always been good to me. As a pastor I've heard horror stories from people who have had awful church experiences. I'm heartbroken over the often-told stories of manipulative pastors, backbiting church members, and embattled church boards. I'm even more grieved knowing the ongoing stories of abuse by pastors and priests. As we engage in the way of community we have to remember that quite a number of people have been hurt by the church. I never had those kind of negative childhood experiences, in part because I was in and out of church as a child. My family didn't really start attending church regularly until I was ten years old. All of my childhood memories of church were positive. I remember the kind people and smiling faces. I remember the sense of community and belonging in the worship services I attended. I followed Jesus into the waters of baptism while in elementary school. Then middle school hit. The changes. The hormones. The awareness of girls. The awareness of my own awkwardness. During middle school I became less interested in church and more interested in sleeping in on Sunday mornings.

A NEW OUTLOOK ON CHURCH

Everything changed when as a teenager I took seriously my vocational call to serve Jesus in full-time ministry. I still carried an unexplainable disdain for organized religion and anything too "churchy," but I couldn't stay away from the church even though I had mixed emotions. The church taught me the Jesus way. I had begun to attend our youth group at a time when quite a number of students were coming to faith. Many of us were serious about our pursuit of Jesus. A group of us were literally at the church every time the doors were open. We would dutifully attend the first service on Sunday mornings, followed by our assigned Sunday school class, and then we'd stay for the second service. I was once asked why I wanted to attend the second service when the sermon was exactly the same. I replied, "Because I don't want to miss anything!" We would return for evening activities including (but not limited to) youth choir, youth drama, youth discipleship, and the Sunday night worship service. I would even stay after the evening service to be a part of the quarterly business meetings. On one occasion we were voting for deacons. I proudly lifted my hand to vote for Fred to serve as a deacon and then I turned to the person next to me and asked, "What's a deacon?" I didn't really care what a deacon was or what a deacon did, I just wanted to be a part of what the church was doing!

That summer I began a love affair with the church that hasn't died. I loved that church because they loved me and accepted me and introduced me to Jesus. As a teenager I enjoyed occasionally rattling the conservative sensibilities of my church. On occasion, I would wear ripped jeans and Birkenstock sandals to church in place of my white shirt and tie. Once I wore a Santa hat to a Sunday night Christmas

program, which infuriated the music minister. I asked difficult questions when practices or doctrines in the church didn't
match the verses in the Bible I was taught to love. These infre-
quent acts of rebellion came from an honest and playful place.
They were never intended to offend. I loved my church. I had
been baptized in that church, learned to love Jesus there, and
during college my wife and I were married in that church.

After college my wife and I moved to Tulsa, Oklahoma,
where I began seminary at Oral Roberts University. My seminary years were a time of tremendous growth for me as I
learned biblical languages. Well, I learned one biblical language—Greek. I dropped Hebrew after six weeks, a mistake
I still regret. My seminary professors introduced me to the
world of historical theology, which gave me a much bigger
view of the global church than just the narrow denomination
of my childhood. I devoured book after book as my heart
opened up to the richness and diversity of Christian tradition.
I loved it, maybe too much. Halfway through my seminary
experience, I wrestled with adding a second master's degree
to the three-year degree I was working on for preparation for
pastoral ministry. I spent a few weeks considering whether or
not to abandon my dreams of vocational ministry in order to
pursue a PhD and devote my life to the academy. The tipping
point in my decision-making was my calling and my love for
the local church. I love the world of academic theology but my
real home is with the people of God in the church. By God's
grace I have been able to serve two churches over nearly two
decades as a pastor.

I have grown to love the church in all of her diversity. I love the Orthodox Church and the Roman Catholic
Church. I love the many mainline Protestant churches and

nondenominational churches. I love evangelical churches and Pentecostal churches. I love Wesleyan/holiness churches and I love Anabaptist churches. I love traditional churches, liturgical churches, and hipster modern churches. I love megachurches and small churches, urban churches and rural churches. I love single-campus churches and multi-site churches. If Jesus is preached where the church is gathered, I will rejoice. If God is worshiped as Father, Son, and Holy Spirit and the gospel of Jesus Christ is proclaimed, I will rejoice. If the Jesus way is pursued and demonstrated and if Scripture is honored in the context of the historic creeds of the faith, then I will rejoice. We are in the same family, worshiping the same God, reading the same Bible, filled with same Holy Spirit, and we are following the same Jesus. He loves us in the uniqueness of our individuality, but he also loves us collectively. Jesus loves his church and so should we. To walk in the ways of Jesus is to walk in the way of community.

MY CHURCH IS JESUS' CHURCH

Church is a public gathering of the baptized followers of Jesus where the gospel is proclaimed and celebrated, the sacraments are observed, and the way of Jesus is modeled and taught. This gathering is the church that Jesus is building and he himself is the head. Paul offers this prayer in his letter to the church in Ephesus:

> I do not cease to give thanks for you, remembering you in my prayers, that the God of our Lord Jesus Christ, the Father of glory, may give you the Spirit of wisdom and of revelation in the knowledge of him, having the eyes of your hearts enlightened, that you may know what is the hope to which he has called you, what are the riches of

his glorious inheritance in the saints, and what is the immeasurable greatness of his power toward us who believe, according to the working of his great might that he worked in Christ when he raised him from the dead and seated him at his right hand in the heavenly places, far above all rule and authority and power and dominion, and above every name that is named, not only in this age but also in the one to come. And he put all things under his feet and gave him as head over all things to the church, which is his body, the fullness of him who fills all in all. (Ephesians 1:16-23)

We should certainly feel like the Christian gathering we are a part of is *our* church because we feel like church is our family. But at the end of the day our church is Jesus' church. We are his body; he is the head.

Church as a gathering reminds us that church is more than an abstract idea. We do believe in a universal church made up of all Christians in all places and times, a large transnational, multicultural family of which we are beloved members. But our membership in the universal church doesn't replace our active participation in the local church. We still need a local gathering to call home. The North American landscape is peppered with all kinds of different churches with different styles, points of emphasis, ways to connect, and forms of church leadership. We easily form in our mind the picture of the perfect church: one that flawlessly lives out the Jesus way, where people never argue or fight, where all are great friends and agree with us on everything. Dietrich Bonhoeffer encourages us to abandon such dreams of the perfect church. He writes, "Only that fellowship which faces such disillusionment, with all its unhappy and ugly aspects, begins to be what it should be in God's sight. . . . The sooner this shock of disillusionment comes to an individual and to a community the better for both."[1] The sooner we give up on our idealistic dreams of the church and accept our local churches for what they are, faults and all, the better.

What is most important in a local church is maintaining a laser-like focus on Jesus, keeping Jesus foremost and central to everything we do. We should worship Jesus in our gatherings and encourage one another in the ways of Jesus. Our church should be a shelter from the storms of our secular age, a hospital for the sick, and a family for the lost and lonely. Jesus is the best hope for our world, and the church embodies that hope through making disciples of the Jesus way. The church doesn't merely *have* a discipleship ministry or program; the church *is* a discipleship ministry. All the activities of the local church work together to form us as followers of Jesus. Worship, groups, classes, ministries, acts of service, and working for social justice all serve as opportunities for us to grow as disciples.

Cornerstone Church in Americus, Georgia, was the first church I served as a staff pastor. This local church experienced a tumultuous church fight in 2004 when I transitioned there from youth pastor to lead pastor. Our pastor had resigned and leadership problems that had been pushed aside came to the forefront. People got angry. Letters and emails were sent. Meetings were held. Arguments ensued. People left. I felt in over my head. As a young, thirty-year-old pastor, I felt like God had pushed me off from shore in a rowboat with seventeen holes in the bottom and I was trying to plug them all at the same time! My recurring mantra during what we affectionately call "the fight of '04" was "*The ministry of Jesus will go on.*" Through the anger and fighting, the tearful goodbyes of people leaving the church, and through the mistakes I and others made, we kept our eyes on Jesus and he brought us through. That church survived and is thriving today not because it's perfect, but because it's a church filled with God's Spirit. It's a church where people have learned to love one another. Even though I serve another congregation these days, a piece of my heart will always be with Cornerstone Church. As this small, rural gathering of Jesus-followers has allowed the Holy Spirit to lead and direct, the Spirit continues to point them to Jesus just as he promised. Jesus said, "When the Spirit of truth comes, he will guide you into all the truth, for he will not speak on his own authority, but whatever he hears he will speak, and he will declare to you the things that are to come. He will glorify me, for he will take what is mine and declare it to you" (John 16:13-14). Our local churches really do belong to Jesus, and if we provide space for the Holy Spirit, we find the Spirit leading us into the glory and brightness of Jesus.

ONE ANOTHERING

One of the most telling reasons why the Christian faith cannot be practiced in isolation is that so many commands in the New Testament require other people. Over fifty times we find instructions to do something to, for, or with one another. These "one another" commands form for us the way of community. Nowhere in this list of commands do we find anything like "put one another in their place," "fix one another," "judge one another," or "force one another to do the right thing." The local gathering isn't the place for subjugating or fixing one another. The local gathering is where we worship Jesus together and encourage each other in the ways of Jesus. We need one another because following Jesus is incarnational. We need real people in our lives on our journey of following Jesus. We need face-to-face conversations and side-by-side encouragement if we are to grow in becoming like Jesus. Walking in the way of community requires walking in the way of love and transformation. Here are seven of the top "one another" commands.

1. Love one another. Jesus said, "This is my commandment, that you love one another as I have loved you. Greater love has no one than this, that someone lay down his life for his friends. You are my friends if you do what I command you" (John 15:12-14). This directive from Jesus, the most frequent of all the "one another" commands, exists as the soil from which all other commands grow and flourish. It's easy in our digital, virtual, synthetic world to like things with a single tap of the finger. It's much harder to love other people in real time sharing the same space with them. In the real world of physical flesh-and-blood people, we have to work hard to love one another with the kind of sacrificial love Jesus demonstrated, the kind of love he commands us to extend to others. We are to love one another with the love whereby God has loved us, a love he demonstrated in Jesus, a love poured out by his Spirit.

Though we love one another both in our local churches and in all different kinds of churches, we believe in only one church. The Nicene Creed offers four distinguishing marks of the church with these words—We believe in *one, holy, catholic*, and *apostolic* church.[2] We hold on to the unity of the church, because even though we see many different denominations and traditions, we are all following the same Jesus. Our history, from the ugly divide of the Eastern Orthodox and Western Roman Catholic Church to the bloody wars between Catholic and Protestant Christians, hasn't served us well. We need to emphasize those things we agree on and learn to disagree respectfully on those things we don't agree on. We need to love all Christians regardless of their tradition or theological convictions.

We also love those Christians of old, those who made up the ancient historic church. Those Jesus-followers who have gone before us are still a part of the church. They are the "cloud of witnesses" in the grandstands cheering us on (Hebrews 12:1). We love and respect the tradition they have passed down to us, but we continue a conversation with them to understand how ancient traditions function in our modern setting. Loving one another includes loving those who came before us, so we remain respectful of the past while following Jesus in the present.

2. Serve one another. In his letter to the Galatians, Paul writes, "For you were called to freedom, brothers. Only do not use your freedom as an opportunity for the flesh, but through love serve one another" (Galatians 5:13). In following Jesus we have received real freedom from past mistakes, past sins, and past guilt. It's a freedom that breaks the unhealthy cycle of death and destruction in our lives. It isn't a freedom to do whatever we want. We are free from the past so we can serve today. We are free so we can reflect God's image into our world by serving one another in the life of the church. We build authentic community in the church when we gather— not to see what we can get out of the church, but rather what we can give. We certainly experience the great reward of being loved and served by others, but we seek to serve and give back just as much as we receive. Imagine if everyone joined together on Sunday to take something away from the worship service. If no one was giving and no one was serving, the church wouldn't last very long. A gathering of all takers and no givers is a surefire way to kill Christian community.

Serving one another within the church also includes hospitality where we make room for outsiders and welcome them into Christian community. Hospitality is the Christian art of opening up space and welcoming people in. We need friends at church on the journey of following Jesus, but we must always guard ourselves from turning the gathering into an exclusive club for insiders. As we are following Jesus in community we need to keep a watchful eye out for new people, because according to Stanley Hauerwas and Will Willimon, Christian community is where God is creating a new family: "We serve the world by showing it something that it is not, namely, a place where God is forming a family out of strangers . . . if we offer ourselves to a truthful story and the community formed by listening to and enacting that story in the church, we will be transformed into people more significant than we could ever have been on our own."[3] Hospitality is how we serve the strangers among us.

3. Be kind to one another. In one of the most densely packed passages about community in the New Testament, Paul exhorts us to "Be kind to one another, [be] tender-hearted" (Ephesians 4:32). Kindness in a country full of outrage and antagonism isn't easy, but community cannot exist without it. Kindness is the physical expression of love within the church. It makes the way of community possible. We have been given a number of ways to show kindness. Here are a few things *not* to do if we want to see kindness flourish: Don't respond to harsh words with harsh words. Don't respond to hate with hate. Don't trade insult for insult. Don't label people before you know them. Don't assume the worst in people. Don't look for faults in other people. Nowhere in the New Testament does it say "and find fault with one another." In fact

Jesus was clear that we should work to get the log out of our own eye before trying to get a speck out of someone else's eye (Matthew 7:3-5). Assume the best in people and allow them to disappoint you. It's better to experience disappointment with people from time to time than to remain overly emotionally guarded and cynical.

Another proven way to walk in kindness in the way of community is to suspend judgment and offer no unsolicited advice. Jesus is the judge. He will sort things out in the end. We can alleviate the pressure of judging when we recognize that judging is Jesus' job, not ours. Our job is to love, serve, and be kind to others and not force our way in and tell other people what they should or should not be doing. We can genuinely love people, spend time with them, and once a relationship has been built, then perhaps they may come asking for advice. Christian community has a place to "teach and admonish one another" (Colossians 3:16), but we do so in the context of a relationship where trust has been solidified. Kindness is the first step in the way of community toward building the kind of relationships where we can teach one another and learn from each other.

4. Forgive one another. Paul's exhortation continues, "Be kind to one another, tenderhearted, forgiving one another, as God in Christ forgave you" (Ephesians 4:32). Without exception, all of us who walk the way of Christian community will be disappointed and hurt at some time by someone in the church. Very often these offenses are misunderstandings, careless mistakes, or situations where expectations were not clearly expressed and agreed upon. Less often these offenses are malicious attacks. In all these cases we are called to forgive. So when we are kind and people disappoint us, when they sin against us, or when they hurt us, we do what Jesus did on the cross. We pray, "Father, forgive them, for they know not what they do" (Luke 23:34). When we have been hurt we can ball up all our pain and launch it back toward those who have hurt us. We can let them have it so that they will hurt like we hurt. But this form of retaliation isn't the Jesus way. We forgive them just as God in Christ forgave us.

Don't misunderstand this command. Forgiveness doesn't mean what they did was okay. Forgiveness doesn't mean we deserved it. It doesn't mean their actions were somehow justifiable or that it was "no big deal." Forgiveness doesn't mean we get tough and deal with it on our own. Forgiveness doesn't mean the pain of the offense automatically goes away or that we allow them to hurt us again. Forgiveness does mean we choose not to retaliate; that we place them in the hands of God, trusting God to do what is fair. This kind of forgiveness in the way of community requires a process of expressing our hurt and giving the offender the opportunity to ask for forgiveness. A process like this one can lead to reconciliation. However, if the offender refuses to admit his or her wrongdoing, and refuses to ask for forgiveness, we can still forgive and choose not to retaliate. Reconciliation in a situation like that one would be unlikely, but as we walk in forgiveness we can be free and healed of the pain over time.

The celebration of holy communion as the centerpiece of Christian worship becomes a way for us to experience forgiveness. When we participate in the communion meal we remind ourselves of our ongoing need for forgiveness. As we come to the table we recognize Jesus' body broken for us and his blood shed for the forgiveness of sins. Communion connects us in a mysterious way to the body and blood of Jesus. Paul asks,

"The cup of blessing that we bless, is it not a participation in the blood of Christ? The bread that we break, is it not a participation in the body of Christ?" (1 Corinthians 10:16). As we experience forgiveness, we are empowered to forgive.

5. Bear one another's burdens. Paul, in his letter to the Galatians, writes, "Bear one another's burdens, and so fulfill the law of Christ" (Galatians 6:2). To bear the burden of another is the way we offer help in the way of community. A couple of years ago, we had a family in our church with a pretty severe financial need. They had experienced loss of employment, and this family was suffering. Another family offered to host a garage sale to help this family and asked for donations. Our family donated some items and the family with the garage sale brought in nearly seven hundred dollars for the family in need. One of the people who donated items offered the dad a job! This beautiful picture shows us what it looks like to help shoulder the load when someone in the community is struggling.

Bearing one another's burdens also includes the command to "confess your sins to one another and pray for one another, that you may be healed" (James 5:16). The best thing you can do with your sin is bring it out of hiding and into the light. That nagging character flaw that continues to trip you up needs to be exposed. Don't ignore it, rationalize, spiritualize, or hide it. Confess it to another person you trust and pray for each other. You can and should confess your sins to God when you are alone, but the Spirit works to form us and heal us when we bring our sins into the light of loving Christian community.

6. Honor one another. Paul echoes Jesus in his command to love one another and then adds something to it: "Love one another with brotherly affection. Outdo one another in showing honor" (Romans 12:10). Instead of seeking honor for yourself, seek to honor other people. When I walk into a room full of people, my attitude shouldn't be "Well, here I am!" My attitude should be more like "Oh, there you are!" Many of us know how to tease one another, make fun of one another, and give each other a hard time. In some ways making jokes at the expense of another is easy. Honor is difficult. It's counterintuitive. The way we honor one another in Christian community is by respecting one another in humility, which includes respecting the leaders who serve our community. This requires that we set aside our agenda so we can get to know someone else. Respect is a matter of acknowledging that the person standing in front of us is a child of God created in the image of God and brimming with worth and dignity.

We won't always agree with everyone on everything, but respect allows us to preserve the unity of the church by seeking understanding. I can respect other people without agreeing with them. If we are discussing matters of faith or politics or family life, I may disagree with their conclusion, but if they are seriously following Jesus, then I can respect their sincerity and the way they went about forming their conclusions. For example, I am a strong advocate for Christian families to participate in the public school system. I have friends who choose private schools, Christian schools, or homeschool as the best option for their children. I may disagree with their path, but if I seek to understand their reasoning, I can respect their decision for educating their children the way they do when they are working to do what is in the best interest of their child.

I know we won't agree on all matters of theology or politics, but we should remain respectful and open to those with whom we disagree. We should discuss these matters and maybe debate them, but we shouldn't ever get sucked into an impassioned argument. We don't have to agree fully with everyone in the Christian family in order to embrace them as brothers and sisters in Christ. To this end, I have removed the phrase "but I don't agree with him (or her) on everything" from the way I speak of others in the church because it is an unnecessary and unhelpful phrase in a theological or political conversation. I can always find something I disagree with if I look hard enough. We will disagree with one another from time to time, but work toward living at peace with everyone, focusing on those things that will build up the church and not tear it down.

7. *Encourage one another.* In sight of the return of Jesus, Paul writes, "Therefore encourage one another and build one another up, just as you are doing" (1 Thessalonians 5:11). Life is hard. We all have to endure difficult days and seasons of life. Our suffering may not always look the same, but we all have our issues, whether we choose to acknowledge them or not. At some point everyone experiences the flow of life working against them, like walking upstream in a swollen creek. Every step requires ten times the normal amount of energy. We are thrown off balance. The physical struggle turns into mental and emotional fatigue. We need to sit and rest a minute, but we are too afraid of being swept away. We need a break. We need some relief. We need encouragement.

Perhaps the best way we can do life together in the way of community is by encouraging one another. As a Christian leader I remind myself that encouraging people is the *second* most important thing I do. The most important thing I do is point people to Jesus, God's kingdom, and God's mission; the next most important thing is to encourage them.

So we should compliment one another and pat each other on the back. Yes, there are times for correction, but we can never outdo one another in encouragement. Never assume you know what is going on in a person's life. Ask questions. Spend time with them. Discover where they are succeeding and encourage them. Discover where they are failing and encourage them not to quit. Don't give a listening ear to third-party gossip. Go straight to the source and find out for yourself. Give people room to fail. Don't blame and accuse, but find ways to encourage. We encounter enough in our world that tears us down. Let's build each other up in words and actions of affirmation.

Church can be a problem. Our history as the people of God isn't stellar. We have a history of violence, corruption, and greed. Whenever church becomes an end unto itself and begins accommodating to the established cultural values where she is planted, the church becomes sick and twisted. But God has been merciful. God has promised never to leave us or forsake us (Hebrews 13:5). God promises to never quit on the church. Let's remained resolved to do the same. We need the local gathering of Jesus-followers to challenge us and encourage us. We need friends at church and we need to learn from those who are not like us. The way of Christian community is how we grow in the faith and how we pass on the faith to the next generation. For followers of Jesus, participation in the life of the local church has become a habit.

discussion **questions**

1. In the past, have you experienced the good, the bad, or the ugly of the church? Or some combination of all three? Explain.

2. What is your church experience like these days?

3. What have you grown to appreciate about other churches or other Christian traditions?

4. What are the key differences between the church *having* a discipleship ministry and the church *being* a discipleship ministry?

5. In what ways have you served your local church?

6. What are some practical ways to practice hospitality at home or at church?

7. Why is unsolicited advice given prior to the establishment of a relationship detrimental to Christian community?

8. Why is it challenging to honor and respect someone with whom we disagree?

9. What is the best way to encourage someone with whom you go to church?

10. How can you begin to pray for your church in a new way this week?

9

Habitus

The Way of Liturgy

I find it sad that when we talk about habits, we normally think of *bad* habits like biting our fingernails, eating more junk food than vegetables, and carrying a balance on our credit cards. I admit that I have been guilty of all of these bad habits from time to time. Some habits can be very destructive. When a habit becomes a compulsion and is detrimental to our well-being, we are in trouble. These habits leave us trapped in a cycle of addiction and we need help to get out. But not all habits are inherently bad. Habits themselves are morally neutral. In fact, the way we break bad and old habits is through the arduous process of forming good and new habits. Bad habits seem to sneak up on us. I don't think I've ever consciously chosen to pick up a bad habit. Over time, through neglect and my own foolishness, I have adopted poor ways of living reinforced by poor habits.

When I was in my mid-thirties my wife Jenni was pregnant with our third child. I remember praying for a daughter before she got pregnant. I felt so incredibly lucky to have two sons, so I asked God for a daughter. But as I sat in front of the grainy screen during the gender-reveal sonogram, I was thrilled to learn God was blessing us with another son. Even though God didn't answer my prayer the way I expected, I was still happy. I knew what to expect with boys, so another one would be relatively easy. Welcoming a new child into the house meant changes—I did remember that. My older boys were nine and ten years old and we hadn't had a baby in the house for quite some time. One of the necessary changes in our home to accommodate our growing family was converting our long, narrow den into a nursery and office. I had some friends help me frame up a wall and hang a door to create a new room for our coming baby boy. Once we hung the drywall on the wood studs, I took to taping and mudding all the seams. The wall was only nine feet wide, and for an experienced drywaller this job would have been both quick and easy. However, I was not experienced and the job of taping and mudding was neither quick nor easy. I learned the process of applying thin coats of joint compound (the "mud"), letting it dry, and then lightly sanding before applying another coat. One night, while sanding a new coat of the white, chalky mud, I took off my long-sleeve shirt and was wearing just a tight-fitting undershirt. Jenni took a picture of the progress, and when I finally had a chance to see the picture, I saw what had become obvious to others. All of those slices of pizza and cheeseburgers, combined with my lack of exercise, were catching up to me. I had been lean and athletic in high school, but I had become terribly out of shape. All that extra weight had gathered around my midsection. The time had come for me to develop some new habits.

I had played basketball with some guys at the gym at our local college once or twice a week, but I wasn't in great physical condition. I ran track and played basketball in high school. I even considered the possibility of running track in college, but those years were far behind me. I was a husband, father, and pastor with a mortgage, two vehicles, and a church to serve. After the birth of our third child, I knew I needed to make a change. My bad habit was a lack of exercise, and I wasn't sure how to break it. I heard of the popular "couch to 5K" training programs. As I scoured the Internet I discovered many different proven plans to move a person from the couch of inactivity to running 3.1 miles, a 5K—which if run at a ten-minute-per-mile pace meant running, nonstop, for just over thirty minutes. My first thought was, "No way." I couldn't imagine how I would be able to run (without stopping) for thirty minutes. Nevertheless, I copied down a twelve-week training schedule and mustered up my half-hearted confidence and gave it a shot.

My first week of training had me walk twenty-five minutes with no running. I skipped that week. The second week had me walking six minutes and running one minute, four times, for a total of twenty-eight minutes over three different days. I thought that was too easy, so I skipped week two and moved right on to week three, which instructed me to walk five minutes and run two minutes four times three days a week. Since this plan had me monitor my walk/run intervals according to time and not distance, I headed over to the local high school to walk and run on the track. I walked fairly quickly, but my two-minute runs were rather slow. "Don't die. Just finish," I kept saying to myself. On the last walk/run of week three, I wanted to challenge myself. On the last run of the last interval on the last training day of the week I decided to double my time and run four minutes instead of two minutes. The sun was beating down on me that day and the air was still and thick. As I crossed over the three-minute mark, my heart was pounding and my legs started feeling like they were being weighed down with bags of concrete. When the stopwatch on my wrist elapsed four minutes, I slowed down and my run turned into a lumbered walk. I found a grassy area under the shade of a tree and lay down. As I tried to catch my breath, I watched my chest rapidly rise and fall. I thought I was going to die.

Fast-forward seven years later and I was crossing the finish line of the Kansas City Marathon in just under five hours. I experienced a tremendous sense of accomplishment in completing a marathon, but how did I go from nearly dying after running four minutes to completing a marathon? The answer is simple—training and the development of new habits. I trained and completed a handful of 5K races. I went on to train for two complete half marathons (13.1-mile races). Then I trained for eighteen weeks for my first marathon, but on race day, uncertainty hung like a dark cloud over me. I had put all of my trust in a training plan that never had me run 26.2 miles. The furthest I had run during my training was twenty-two miles. Would I be able to finish all twenty-six miles? I had run four days a week for eighteen weeks in the rain, in the heat, in the humidity, and on vacation while in sunny Florida. I had run early in the morning before the sun came up; I had run under the stars at night. As I was nearing the twenty-mile mark during my marathon, I had settled into a good running pace and I realized that the training had prepared me for that exact moment. I knew I was going to make it. The training I had doubted in the beginning carried me through to the finish line!

The distance of my training runs varied, but I ran every Monday, Wednesday, Friday, and Saturday. I didn't decide on these days if I was going to run; I just ran. It had become a habit. In order to reach my goal, I needed to trust the wisdom of those who had come before me and follow their lead. I had to trust the training plan I was given, set aside my concerns, and commit myself to train in the way laid out for me. When I settled into the training, long-distance running became a habit, a good one, and that simple habit turned me into a marathon runner. Habits are simple and mundane. Accomplishing goals is thrilling! The four-day-a-week habit of running is rather boring. But crossing the finish line after running 26.2 miles is exhilarating! Welcoming the boredom associated with our habits becomes key in reaching our goals. Becoming like Jesus fully at home in the trinitarian life of God is thrilling. The steps to get there can be monotonous. To be honest, sometimes following Jesus is boring. *Welcome the boredom.* Sometimes following Jesus is repetitive. *Accept the routine.* Sometimes following Jesus is quiet. *Cherish the silence.* Sometimes following Jesus is slow. *Embrace the pace.* We need Christian habits to form us in this new pace of life in pursuit of Jesus.

HABITS THAT LEAD TO *HABITUS*

When we form new habits as followers of Jesus, we discover God will use these habits to form something new in us. These habits have the power to shape us if we are willing to reject the idea that novelty is the way to life. We live in a culture energized by entertainment. We have been conditioned by social media to expect a constant flow of new images and information. Every time we tap a social media app on our phones we receive something new—new pictures, a new status, new links, new opinions, or new videos. Forming good habits as a follower of Jesus means growing comfortable with routines. Accepting as normal the human practice of doing the same things over and over. Social media stimulates and captures our attention, but slowly and progressively it's creating in us a distaste for routine and repetitive habits. To pray the same prayers, to read the same Scriptures, to celebrate the same holy days becomes boring, not because there isn't life to be found in these habits, but because we have been conditioned to desire something new, something novel.

On this road following Jesus, we will learn and begin to practice new habits which, when enlivened by God's Spirit, will drive out old habits. These habits can be gathered together under two different labels: "habits of the heart" and "habits of training." These two distinct kinds of habits have a great deal of overlap, but the way we practice them is different. They share in common the same goal: *habitus*. This strange little Latin word refers to the inward dispositions that drive us. Think of *habitus* as the instincts that give birth to our choices and behaviors. Alan Kreider describes *habitus* as formed by the way we do what we do, a kind of knowledge carried in our bodies. For Kreider, *habitus* "constitutes our profoundest sense of identity; that forms our deepest convictions, allegiances, and repulsions; and that shapes our response to ultimate questions—what will we live for, die for, and kill (or not kill) for."[1] The ongoing practice of Christian habits, whether the ones of the heart or the ones of training, produces within us a kind of holy *habitus*, or character. In this way we accept habits as gifts from followers of Jesus who have gone before us, habits that seek to form a certain kind of character within us. We practice Christian habits in order to form a Christian *habitus* within us.

The habits of the heart include those things we do in order to be formed in the Christlike character we desire as followers of Jesus. In other words, if we want to be patient people then we form habits of patience in which we do patient things like waiting quietly in the checkout line at the grocery store. If we desire to be people of a strong work ethic, we develop such character by making it a habit to work hard. These habits reflect what the Greek philosopher Aristotle, who lived 350 years before Jesus, taught about virtue and character. According to Aristotle, "Moral virtue comes about as a result of habit. . . . The virtues we get by first exercising them, as also happens in the case of the arts as well. For the things we have to learn before we can do them, we learn by doing them, e.g., men become builders by building and lyre-players by playing the lyre; so too we become just by doing just acts, temperate by doing temperate acts, brave by doing brave acts."[2] Peter echoes this idea of practicing these habits of the heart until they are formed in us when he writes, "For this very reason, make every effort to supplement your faith with virtue, and virtue with knowledge, and knowledge with self-control, and self-control with steadfastness, and steadfastness with godliness, and godliness with brotherly affection, and brotherly affection with love. . . . Therefore, brothers, be all the more diligent to confirm your calling and election, for if you *practice these qualities* you will never fall" (2 Peter 1:5-7, 10, emphasis mine). We supplement these qualities of our faith when we practice them.

These habits take time to cultivate, because we all follow a similar progression toward perfection in Christian character.

This progression toward competency in the habits of the heart looks like this:

1. We are ignorant of our ignorance.
2. We are conscious of our ignorance.
3. We are consciously competent.
4. We are unconsciously competent.

We all begin in the same place. First, *we are ignorant of our ignorance*. We don't know what we don't know. In this state we are unaware of what comprises Christian character or why we should obtain it. This first state is the saddest of all because not only do we lack the character of Christ, we don't even know what we are missing! Second, *we are conscious of our ignorance*. As we employ the four practices in the way of resurrection (awareness, learning, reflecting, action), we become aware of what we did not know and we start to learn the way of Jesus. We suddenly have the realization that we don't know what a heart like Jesus looks like or what new habits we should practice. Third, *we are consciously competent*. Now we have arrived at the place where we know the kind of character we want, the kind of character exemplified in Jesus, and we also know the habits we need to practice in order to form such character within us. But we have to constantly remind ourselves to practice the habits. Fourth, *we are unconsciously competent*. At this stage we have formed a new *habitus*. The character or virtue we have been seeking has become instinctual and we can act without the work of consciously thinking about it.[3]

The primary Christian habits of the heart which we practice are faith, hope, and love. Faith includes acknowledging what is true about God and God's world in statements of belief. *I believe God is the creator. I believe Jesus is God's Son and our*

Lord. I believe God is love. I believe Jesus died for our sins and rose from the dead. These statements of belief then get translated into actions that demonstrate our trust. In other words, we live in a way that only makes sense if what we believe is true. I can claim to believe that a chair is designed to hold my body weight, but I don't really believe it until I demonstrate my trust in the chair's construction and actually sit in it. Hope is the expectation that God will in fact create order out of disorder by making all things right. Christian hope is the triumph of a Jesus-rooted confidence over soul-crushing despair. When we exercise hope we refuse to give in to the evil and destruction around us, knowing that God's good creation will not be lost, but God will, in the end, erase evil from the pages of humanity and remake a new world. The greatest of these Christian virtues is love. God created us in God's very image and nature, so that when we love one another, when we love the weak and the most vulnerable among us, when we love our enemies, we become who we were created to be.

HABITS OF TRAINING

We cannot reduce following Jesus simply to following a handful of rules, but we do need some rules. We may not like the sound of "rules and regulations." They may seem too restrictive, too limiting for us. Rules can have the negative effect of stirring up guilt or shame within us when we fail to follow them. We need rules not so we stay out of trouble, but for our formation. Rules provide healthy boundaries for us as we follow Jesus. Without them we lose our sense of purpose.

Imagine trying to play a board game without rules. My boys and I love playing all sorts of games and Monopoly has always been a favorite. *Can you imagine what it would be like to play Monopoly with no rules?* If there were no rules regarding what direction to move your token, no rules concerning how many spaces to advance around the board, and no rules on what happens when you land on "Free Parking," what would be the point of the game? (You know you are supposed to get all the money in the center of the board, right?!?) The rules we need as followers of Jesus aren't a collection of strict moral codes. Jesus has given us commands to obey, summed up in the big two mandates to love God and love neighbor. The rules that will shape the character of Jesus in us are more like time-tested practices that create order in our lives. Pete Scazzero calls these practices a "Rule of Life." According to Scazzero, "A Rule of Life, very simply, is an intentional, conscious plan to keep God at the center of everything we do. It provides guidelines to help us continually remember God as the Source of our lives."[4] This Rule of Life contains the habits of training. It's the way of liturgy.

The word *liturgy* comes from a Greek word most often translated "service" in the New Testament. For example, when Paul praises the financial generosity of God's people he writes, "For the ministry of this service [liturgy] is not only supplying the needs of the saints but is also overflowing in many thanks-givings to God" (2 Corinthians 9:12). We can best translate *liturgy* as "the work of the people." It has come to denote the scripted forms of worship, both in our personal habits, like liturgies of prayer, as well as our public habits, like the liturgies of worship on Sunday morning. While a growing number of Christians have been working to create new liturgies, the strength of the way of liturgy is found in activating the liturgies found in the great tradition handed down to us by Christians from centuries ago. We shouldn't regard tradition with suspicion, assuming traditions are "dead." As historian Jaroslav Pelikan has noted, "Tradition is the living faith of the dead, traditionalism is the dead faith of the living. And, I suppose I should add, it is traditionalism that gives tradition such a bad name."[5] To see traditional liturgies as an end in themselves leads to traditionalism and thus a dead faith. But to incorporate tradition into an active life of pursuing Jesus is to bring the living faith of the past into our present.

PERSONAL HABITS: PRAYER AND SCRIPTURE

The personal habits of training begin with prayer. Christians from the beginning have followed Jesus' example of prayer. The four biographers of Jesus note how Jesus integrated prayer into his life. For example, "And rising very early in the morning, while it was still dark, he departed and went out to a desolate place, and there he prayed" (Mark 1:35). Jesus prayed not in order to accomplish something, but to remain attentive to God whom he called Father. As he told his parents, when as a boy they found him in the temple listening to the teachers, he wanted to be about his Father's business. If we desire to follow Jesus into the business of being fully human, we too need to practice the habit of prayer. Jesus taught us not to turn prayer into a public spectacle, but, Jesus said, "when you pray, go into your room and shut the door and pray to your Father who is in secret" (Matthew 6:6). Prayer is how we make space for God. Prayer is how we hit pause on the noise and busyness of our day to become aware of God's presence in and among us. Jesus continued by adding, "And your Father who sees in secret will reward you" (Matthew 6:6). The reward God gives in prayer is the gift of becoming ourselves, the gift of finding our true selves in connection to God. Prayer doesn't change *things* as much as prayer changes *us*. This kind of praying requires a liturgy.

When the original followers of Jesus asked him to teach them how to pray, Jesus didn't give them a twelve-point lecture series on the importance of prayer. Jesus didn't give them seven "golden keys" to unlocking a successful prayer life. Instead Jesus gave them a liturgy, a scripted form of prayer. Jesus said to them, "When you pray, say . . ." (Luke 11:2). What he gave them has become known as the Lord's Prayer, which offers a wonderful pattern for prayer, and it's a prayer to both memorize and pray:

> *Our Father, who art in heaven,*
> *hallowed be thy name,*
> *thy kingdom come,*
> *thy will be done,*
> *on earth as it is in heaven.*
> *Give us this day our daily bread.*
> *And forgive us our trespasses,*
> *as we forgive those who trespass against us.*
> *And lead us not into temptation,*
> *but deliver us from evil.*
> *For thine is the kingdom,*
> *and the power,*
> *and the glory, for ever.*
> *Amen.*

The earliest Christians prayed this prayer three times a day. If prayed slowly it takes only thirty seconds to pray. Learning to pray this prayer multiple times a day is the first step in the way of liturgy.

I freely admit that for a long time prayer was a struggle for me. My life of prayer would come and go; even today I struggle with consistency. What has helped me more than anything else is learning to lean into a liturgy of prayer. I learned Brian Zahnd's morning liturgy of prayer which he calls a "track of prayer." This liturgy isn't lifeless, but life giving and deeply formative. According to Zahnd, "It's not a recitation of rote words; it's a liturgy brimming with life. It's not empty; it's full of sacred truth. It's not dry; it's as fresh as the Holy Spirit. It's not self-expression, but formative prayer."[6] I took his liturgy and I made some alterations to form "A Morning Prayer Liturgy" of my own. Devoting myself to this liturgy of prayer has caused me to grow in prayer like nothing else I have ever tried. (See the appendix for the complete prayer liturgy.) When I pray in the morning, I pray nearly the same thing, using the same words. Some prayers change from day to day or week to week and the liturgy gives me space to pray every day from my heart. We should make our requests known to God, but if all we do is ask God to give us things and do things for us, we run the risk of turning God into an errand boy whom we send off to fulfill our wandering desires. According to Brian Zahnd, "The primary purpose of prayer is not to get God to do what we think God ought to do, but to be properly formed."[7] A liturgy of prayer gives us space to "cry out" to God and pray anything we want to pray, but the morning prayer liturgy surrounds these prayers of intercession and petition with well-crafted, time-tested prayers from the church.

The second and equally foundational habit of training is devotion to reading Scripture. The Bible, written by human authors and inspired by the Holy Spirit, gives shape and direction to us as we follow Jesus. We believe "every part of Scripture is God-breathed and useful one way or another—showing us truth, exposing our rebellion, correcting our mistakes, training us to live God's way. Through the Word we are put together and shaped up for the tasks God has for us" (2 Timothy 3:16-17 *The Message*). We read the Bible, all of it, as a way to point us to Jesus and the Jesus way. Jesus himself said, "You search the Scriptures because you think that in them you have eternal life; and it is they that bear witness about me" (John 5:39). Reading, studying, and even memorizing parts of Scripture is an indispensable habit for followers of Jesus. Ancient Christians have given us sacred Scripture as our story, the storied people of God. We read these God-breathed words with great attention, allowing them to guide us in the Jesus way. In order to do this, we need a Jesus-centered reading of the Bible where we seek how all of the Bible points us to Jesus. This approach to reading Scripture has been a strength of the Anabaptist tradition. According to Stuart Murray, Anabaptists historically have "insisted that the Bible must be interpreted in light of the life, death, and resurrection of Jesus Christ. Jesus was the center of the Bible, the one to whom both Testaments pointed."[8] While reading Scripture, the recurring question is "How does what I am reading lead me to Jesus?"

Bible reading in a Jesus-centered way requires not only reading the words on the page but understanding them in a way that remains faithful to the ways of Jesus. In the words of the fourth-century church father Hilary of Poitiers, "Scripture is not in the reading, but in the understanding."[9] We should read on our own and work toward understanding in community. We need the help of other followers of Jesus, both the ones in our local church and the ones who dedicate their lives as scholars wrestling with Scripture. A helpful guide toward a Jesus-centered understanding of the Bible is what has been called the "Wesleyan Quadrilateral." Inspired by the writing and preaching of John Wesley from the eighteenth century, this form of reflection includes four components: Scripture, tradition, reason, and experience. This way of reading and understanding Scripture grew out of a very individualized culture, but it's a helpful guide when practiced in community. We can use it to wrestle together to grasp who God is as revealed in Jesus and what God is doing in the world.

We start by honoring Scripture as our sacred text. We learn the great tradition of the church with its ancient roots and allow the early church's prayers, sermons, and creeds to help us. We employ the reason God has given us and allow our minds to be shaped by scholars and seasoned teachers in the church. We allow the Holy Spirit to give us a real encounter with the God of Scripture. We allow the gathering of Jesus-followers around us to give shape to all four of these components, because the Bible itself was written by a community, about a community, for a community. Prayer and Scripture reading are not the only personal habits of Jesus-followers, but they form the twin pillars upon which all the other habits rest.[10]

PUBLIC HABITS: WORSHIP

Following Jesus is personal, but never private. Even the personal habits of prayer and Scripture reading are reinforced by a community. Jesus didn't call isolated individuals, encouraging them to have a private relationship with him and then go back to their homes and try to do Jesus things all by themselves. From the beginning Jesus worked to form a community. When Peter declared publicly that Jesus was the Christ, that is, the Jewish king coming to announce the arrival of the kingdom, Jesus said, "And I tell you, you are Peter, and on this rock I will build my church, and the gates of hell shall not prevail against it" (Matthew 16:18). Jesus has been building his church as little (and sometimes big) gatherings scattered all over the earth. The day will come when Jesus will appear and make all things right. Until then we need not be "neglecting to meet together, as is the habit of some, but encouraging one another, and all the more as you see the Day drawing near" (Hebrews 10:25). From the beginning, Christians have gathered together on Sundays to mark the resurrection of Jesus. In the time before Jesus, the people of God set aside Saturday as a Sabbath day, where instead of work they would devote themselves to worship. The resurrection of Jesus was such a momentous event that Jewish followers of Jesus moved the day of worship from Saturday to Sunday, the traditional first day of the week. Today some Christians choose to gather for worship on different days, which is completely acceptable. To worship on Sunday has been the tradition of the church, but the important question is not when we gather for worship, but whether we fully engage in worship when we are gathered with other followers of Jesus.

Each local church has its own traditions and style. Choosing a church community to worship with is a personal choice. I compare choosing local churches to choosing a potential spouse: pick one and love that one for the rest of your life. Don't get trapped in the endless cycle of looking for the perfect church. It doesn't exist. All of us on this journey of following Jesus have areas of our lives that haven't yet been conformed into the likeness of Jesus. We all depend on God's grace and mercy. We're all striving to grow in Christlikeness. We gather together to worship God and encourage one another. While our ways of worship differ, nearly all church worship services have songs to sing, prayers to pray, Scriptures to be read and expounded upon, and communion to be celebrated. We come to sing because God reigns. We come to pray because God hears. We come to Scripture because God speaks. We come to the communion table because God saves. We participate in these activities not to evaluate how we feel or to "get something out of it." We participate in weekly worship to put ourselves in a place of training and formation, where we can experience the shaping of the Spirit.

Nothing grounds us in the love of God more than the practice of holy communion. Your church may celebrate communion (also called "the Lord's Supper" or "the eucharist") weekly, monthly, or a couple times a year. Jesus gives us an opportunity to commune with him every time we eat and drink at the communion table. Jesus called himself the bread of God come into the world to give his life to the world. He said, "The bread that I will give for the life of the world is my flesh" (John 6:51). He established this practice in his final meal with his disciples before his death. He took bread and after blessing it, broke it and gave it saying, "Take, eat; this is my body" (Matthew 26:26). Likewise he took a cup and after giving thanks he gave it to his disciples and said, "Drink of it, all of you, for this is my blood of the covenant, which is poured out for many for the forgiveness of sins" (Matthew 26:27-28). In that moment Jesus gave us the clearest picture of what his death on the cross was all about. His death demonstrated God's faithfulness to the covenant God made with Abraham to bless and rescue all of the families of the earth. God's faithfulness brought the forgiveness of sins, cleansing and liberating God's people from enslavement to sin, death, and all the ways of empire.

The sacraments of communion and baptism contain symbols, but they are more than symbolic. As Gordon Smith notes, "The sacraments are not mere tokens. They are the very means by which the church lives; the life of the church depends on them. They are crucial to our commitment to spiritual formation and discipleship."[11] We receive holy communion so we can be formed in holiness as the people of God, walking in the footsteps of King Jesus. When we participate in communion, we remember the death of Jesus. We proclaim the presence of forgiveness. We confess both our sins and our allegiance to King Jesus afresh and anew. This liturgical act forms our identity as followers of Jesus as we discover we are blessed, broken, and given for the sake of God's mission in the world.[12] At the table we are reminded of our mission as the people of God to join in God's rescue and justice in a world set adrift without a moral center.

We all have bad habits. If we are honest, we'll admit we each have bad habits in the way we communicate, the way we think, the way we act, or in the way we interact with others. The only way to break bad habits is to form new habits. Putting new habits of the heart and habits of training into practice is like a farmer putting seeds into the ground. The harvest from such habits is a *habitus*, a character-based instinct that guides what we do. We need our minds renewed so that we have the mind of Christ, but we primarily don't do what we *know* we should do. More often than not we do what we *want* to. Our desires are shaped by the *habitus* living within us and reinforced by the way of liturgy. These habits form us into the people God wants us to be for the sake of his mission in the world.

discussion **questions**

1. What are some bad habits you have overcome? How did you break them?

2. How would you describe *habitus* in your own words?

3. Have you experienced the formation of certain character traits by practicing them? Explain.

4. Describe a time when you have become unconsciously competent, when you have so mastered a skill that you can do it without thinking about it.

5. What value have you found in the traditions of the church?

6. What is your prayer life like today? How do you think a liturgy of scripted prayer may help you?

7. What steps can you take in order to let your Bible reading lead you to Jesus?

8. What parts of worship do you find the most difficult to engage in? What can you do to overcome that difficulty?

9. What has your experience with communion been like?

10. What new habits can you start this week to begin to form new character traits in your heart?

10

Justice

The Way of Reconciliation

Hell kindles its flames in the days of war. When I read the words of Jesus describing a frightful place of outer darkness, weeping, and gnashing of teeth, an awful place where the "worm does not die and the fire is not quenched" (Mark 9:48), I think of clouds of fiery-red napalm burning the jungle and thatch-roof huts ablaze during the Vietnam War. I think of brave men dressed in green carrying wounded soldiers through tall grass and Vietnamese children screaming in terror.[1] War encapsulates everything wrong with our world. The destruction, hate, violence, misery, and death, followed by PTSD, despair, suicide, and lingering pain, all represent the brokenness of the world God loves. I've never seen a battlefield, but my father has. My dad served one tour in Vietnam in 1970, four years before I was born. He's a decorated veteran who received multiple Purple Hearts and a Bronze Star. By God's grace he passed through the flames of hell.

In light of my dad's military service, my first trip to the Vietnam Veterans Memorial in Washington, D.C., turned out to be more emotional than I expected. It was a sunny April day when I stepped off the Metro and up the stairs out of the Smithsonian Station and onto the sidewalk on the outskirts of the National Mall in D.C. With map in hand I plotted my course to see the sights, knowing the Vietnam Veterans Memorial would be a real highlight for me. What I didn't prepare for was the deluge of emotions I would experience. I walked up and around the imposing Washington Monument and took the obligatory pictures. I continued on and passed the popular World War II Memorial. I saw a young couple taking selfies next to what I assumed was their home state's stone pillar. Families with little children walked and played in the monument area as I continued my walk. I followed a pebble stone path through the grass on my way to the Vietnam Veterans Memorial. Through the trees on my left I could see the reflecting pool and I enjoyed a few moments of quiet and isolation. In my mind I prepared my plan. I knew I didn't have time to read each of the over fifty-eight thousand names of the Americans who died during the Vietnam War, but I was determined to look at each of the seventy black granite panels that comprised the wall.

As I approached the memorial I could see that the panels were dug into a grassy hill. The cobblestone path began to descend and I looked to my right to see the first of the black granite panels, a short one that seemed to rise out of the ground. The first few panels only had a few names on them and didn't even come up to my knee, but I saw them. I continued walking down the path, slowing my pace. The granite wall grew taller as I descended, and the list of names per panel grew more numerous. As I reached the middle where the memorial takes a turn to the left, the wall reached well over my head. I continued to walk, overwhelmed by the growing number of names of Americans, young and old, who died in the war. I felt my throat tighten and a rush of emotions flooded my body. The bright sun couldn't stop the deathly chill running down my back. I stopped to wipe tears that had begun to form in my eyes. I asked myself silently, "Will we ever learn? How many more people have to die before we will learn the ways of peace? How long will we ignore Jesus' warning that those who live by the sword, die by the sword? How long will we reject Jesus' teachings on forgiveness, peace, and love? How long will the drums of war continue to resound and keep us captive?" More panels and more names came and I wanted to run, but I forced myself to walk slowly. I allowed the multiplied thousands of names to assault my imagination. As I finished my slow walk, and with the wall behind me, I found a bench near the statue of three Vietnam War soldiers. With the weight of my worried mind, I sat taking in a deep breath of God's fresh air. I prayed a brief prayer and then I called my dad.

With my heart still burdened by the nearly sixty thousand names forever etched in black granite, I walked on to the Lincoln Memorial where the stoic Lincoln sat enshrined in his "temple." I walked around in Lincoln's temple, unimpressed. I said farewell to Lincoln and walked out of the entryway where I stumbled on the phrase "I HAVE A DREAM" etched into the stone floor. I remembered this was the very spot where Dr. Martin Luther King Jr. stood and delivered his famous speech inviting people to imagine a world free of racial injustice. My troubled thoughts were locked in on the Vietnam War, but I suddenly remembered Dr. King and thought to myself, "Where is his memorial?" I consulted my map and quickly trotted down the stairs with Lincoln behind me and with a subtle sadness settling into my heart. I passed the ominous Korean War Veterans Memorial, crossed the busy street, and headed toward the Martin Luther King Jr. Memorial. I entered through the back side of the memorial, through the passage-way created through what looked to be the reconstruction of a mini-mountain, the mountain of despair. I walked around the large thirty-foot piece of white granite that seemed to have been pushed forward from the mountain. As I made my way around, I could see the man of peace himself, Dr. King, the stone of hope, a prophet who spoke to the powers that be, a prophet filled with love in his heart. I took another deep breath.

Behind the large granite relief of Dr. King were quotations from his speeches etched into the back wall. Just as I walked past each of the black granite panels in the Vietnam Veterans Memorial, I took my time to walk purposefully and read the words of Dr. King. As I did, I could hear his voice in my head and slowly all the sadness and unsettledness I felt began to disappear. I read lines like these:

> "*We shall overcome because the arc of the moral universe is long, but it bends toward justice.*"

> "*I believe that unarmed truth and unconditional love will have the final word in reality. This is why right, temporarily defeated, is stronger than evil triumphant.*"

> "*I oppose the war in Vietnam because I love America. I speak out against it not in anger but with anxiety and sor-row in my heart, and above all with a passionate desire to see our beloved country stand as a moral example of the world.*"

"Injustice anywhere is a threat to justice everywhere. We are caught in an inescapable network of mutuality, tied in a single garment of destiny. Whatever affects one directly, affects all indirectly."

"It is not enough to say 'We must not wage war.' It is necessary to love peace and sacrifice for it. We must concentrate not merely on the negative expulsion of war, but the positive affirmation of peace."

"True peace is not merely the absence of tension; it is the presence of justice."[2]

These words seemed to wash away all the dirt and grime of war from my imagination. They began to sweep all of the despair out of my heart, and where the hellishness of war had stirred up cynicism within me, Dr. King's words planted seeds of hope. Though war continues to haunt the human psyche, the words of the peacemaker ring true. The arc of the moral universe may be long and seemingly never-ending, but it does indeed bend toward justice.

JUSTICE'S BEAUTIFUL FACE

The healing I found for my heart that day in Washington, D.C., could be summed up in the word *justice*. For the longest time I assumed that word was synonymous with what I understood as law enforcement. This cartoonish understanding of justice envisioned the perpetual cycle of bad guys doing bad things and good guys catching the bad guys and putting them in jail. For me this immature picture of justice stood next to my understanding of the rule of law. If a person broke the law, the result would be justice. My privileged upbringing shaped this limited view of justice, as I grew up in a predominately

white, middle-class, middle-of-America environment where
the waters of justice were rolling down to sweep away the
lawbreakers "out there," far away from the safety of my comfortable suburban life. In the years before my trip to D.C.,
I came to learn what Jesus meant by the word *justice*, often
translated as "righteousness" in the New Testament. I discovered that *justice* is a deeply-rooted biblical word that has more
to do with God setting the world right than God punishing
evildoers. As Cornel West has often repeated, "Justice is what
love looks like in public."

This way of loving in public is what God requires of us.
"He has told you, O man, what is good; and what does the
Lord require of you but to do justice, and to love kindness,
and to walk humbly with your God?" (Micah 6:8). Jesus challenged the Pharisees to pursue the important matters of the
law: things like justice and mercy because they demonstrate
our faithfulness to God, whose heart is bent toward the poor,
the rejected, the oppressed, the marginalized, and the outcast.
Jesus himself proclaimed the gospel according to Isaiah saying,
"The Spirit of the Lord is upon me, because he has anointed
me to proclaim good news to the poor. He has sent me to
proclaim liberty to the captives and recovering of sight to the
blind, to set at liberty those who are oppressed" (Luke 4:18).

God gave the law to his people in the Old Testament to
form and shape them into a people who would rightly love
God in acts of worship and rightly love neighbors in acts of
justice. Jesus himself came not to abolish and disconnect us
from the law and prophets, but to fulfill them. Jesus came as
the "end of the law" (Romans 10:4), that is, the termination
point or full and final flourishing of the law, which is good and
holy. The law had the specific role as temporary guardian until

Jesus came (Galatians 3:24). Jesus shows us how to understand and live out the law of God, and his demonstration is built on what the law and the prophets have to say.

One of the pictures Jesus paints to describe justice is that of grapevines bearing their fruit. Jesus said, "I am the true vine, and my Father is the vinedresser. Every branch in me that does not bear fruit he takes away, and every branch that does bear fruit he prunes, that it may bear more fruit" (John 15:1-2). Jesus made clear that his disciples should grow in knowledge and wisdom by learning from him. They should expect the Holy Spirit to come that they may be "clothed with power from on high" (Luke 24:49), so that by the Spirit's power they may be formed into Christlike people. Jesus designed all of this learning and formation to work together so that followers of Jesus would "bear much fruit and so *prove to be my disciples*" (John 15:8, emphasis mine). We announce to the world we are disciples by love. We prove we are disciples by bearing fruit. *What kind of fruit is Jesus talking about?*

Jesus takes this fruit-bearing imagery from the prophets, particularly Isaiah, who lived more than five hundred years before Jesus. In warning God's people of pending judgment, Isaiah compares the covenant people of God to a vineyard. He images God singing to his people with these words, "Let me sing for my beloved my love song concerning his vineyard: My beloved had a vineyard on a very fertile hill" (Isaiah 5:1). As the poetic words from Isaiah continue, he speaks of the vineyard owner planting the best vines and preparing a vat to make the best wine, but there's a problem. When the owner checks the grapes, he finds wild grapes unsuitable for making wine; the result is that the vineyard will be torn down. Isaiah pulls back the curtain and tell us what the vineyard is and what the fruit of the vine represents: "For the vineyard of the Lord of hosts is the house of Israel, and the men of Judah are his pleasant planting; and he looked for justice, but behold, bloodshed; for righteousness, but behold, an outcry!" (Isaiah 5:7). The fruit God looked for was justice. Jesus tells his followers the same thing. We prove we are followers of Jesus by doing justice, walking in the ways of reconciliation.

GOD'S MISSION

Jesus came to set free what had been enslaved and mend what had been broken, because God empowered Jesus with the Holy Spirit to take the broken parts of our world and put them back together again. This way of reconciliation is what the prophets of old and Jesus himself mean by justice. When we do justice, love kindness, and walk humbly with God, we participate with God in the redemption of the world, fulfilling the mission for which Jesus came. Christopher Wright describes God's mission as a work in which we are invited to participate: "Mission, from the point of view of our human endeavor, means the committed participation of God's people in the purposes of God for the redemption of the whole creation. The mission is God's. The marvel is that God invites us to join in."[3] Jesus invites us to join God in God's works of redemption, making right a world gone wrong. When we bear the fruit of Jesus in the world, we strap on our tool belt and tighten up our boots to go to work with God. Justice is the mission of God. It's the task of the church to make disciples fit for this mission, set upon the all-important work of reconciliation.

Jesus intends to repair the tear in the social fabric of our world. Isaiah looked forward to the time when "The wolf and the lamb shall graze together; the lion shall eat straw like the ox, and dust shall be the serpent's food" (Isaiah 65:25). This age of radical reconciliation, an age where we are called to not hurt or destroy one another, came rushing into the world through Jesus' life, death, resurrection, and ascension. The lingering divisions between men and women, social classes, and ethnic groups have all been overcome so that in Jesus "there is neither Jew nor Greek, there is neither slave nor free, there is no male and female, for you are all one in Christ Jesus" (Galatians 3:28). All forms of exploitation, domination, and exclusion have been defeated by Jesus. As people of justice in the way of reconciliation, we invite people to enter into this kingdom and experience the restoration and transformation of King Jesus.

The Latin phrase for this kind of reconciliation is *e pluribus unum*, "out of the many, one," one of the traditional mottos of the United States. What the American experiment has tried to do has already been accomplished in Jesus. David Fitch believes if we don't see reconciliation actively occurring in the church, then we have lost the way of the gospel. He writes, "Reconciliation is at the core of what God has done and is doing in the world in and through Jesus Christ. . . . Reconciliation is so central to the good news of what God has done in Christ that to see no reconciliation in our churches suggests there is no gospel in them. Reconciliation marks our presence in the world."[4] As the people of God, we work for reconciliation and we model reconciliation as we do justice.

A PEOPLE OF PEACE

We have followed Jesus into a new world where we have become new people with a new perspective and a new mission. "Therefore, if anyone is in Christ, he is a new creation.

The old has passed away; behold, the new has come. All this is from God, who through Christ reconciled us to himself and gave us the ministry of reconciliation; that is, in Christ God was reconciling the world to himself, not counting their trespasses against them, and entrusting to us the message of reconciliation" (2 Corinthians 5:17-19). When we enter into a reconciled relationship with God we tread upon the ground of peace where a relationship once contentious is joyful again. God has reconciled us to him because we were the feisty ones. We are now at peace with God and we share in a new ministry and message. We have become what N. T. Wright calls the "reconciled reconcilers."[5] We encourage people to believe the good news and be reconciled to God. We invite people to join us in following Jesus to experience this new life. Our ministry also extends toward fostering reconciliation between people, working for those things that make for peace.

When Jesus entered the holy city of Jerusalem before his crucifixion, he wept, saying to himself, "Would that you, even you, had known on this day the things that make for peace! But now they are hidden from your eyes" (Luke 19:42). In Jesus' day Jerusalem was an unsettled city, pulsating with threats of violent revolution. Within a generation Rome would lay siege and utterly destroy the city just as Jesus warned. The people of Jerusalem didn't know the things that make for peace. Some two thousand years later we haven't come to know these things either. After two world wars, the advent of nuclear weapons, the bloody Vietnam War, countless modern wars, and the never-ending war on terrorism, we still haven't learned the things that make for peace. As long as we believe fighting and violence will solve our problems, we remain in the darkness of the old world, the world that is passing away. Reconciliation between nations on a large scale and reconciliation between squabbling family members on a small scale require peace, not just the absence of conflict. Jesus pronounced a blessing on the peacemakers, those who hear his words and do them, those who would have the audacity to build their lives on things like enemy-love, radical generosity, and seeking first God's kingdom.

Jesus' teaching on peace came as the fulfillment of the prophecies of old. Isaiah wrote, "'Come, let us go up to the mountain of the Lord, to the house of the God of Jacob, that he may teach us his ways and that we may walk in his paths.' For out of Zion shall go forth the law, and the word of the Lord from Jerusalem. He shall judge between the nations, and shall decide disputes for many peoples; and they shall beat their swords into plowshares, and their spears into pruning hooks; nation shall not lift up sword against nation, neither shall they learn war anymore" (Isaiah 2:3-4).

Let's not wait. Jesus is King now, so let's climb Mount Zion. Others have gone before us and have blazed the trail of peace for us. Let's work for peace in our families, neighborhoods, communities, and the nation where we live. The way of reconciliation and peacemaking is difficult, and people may not understand. They will question us and mock us and say it's impossible. They will ask, "Why are you doing this? Why climb the mountain when we have to live in the valley?" The climb up the mountain of peace is challenging, but we were designed by God to live there. Only on the mountaintop can we see things from a different point of view. From the height of the summit we can see that our enemies are brothers and sisters who bear the image of God. The climb is hard, but we'll tell people, "Wait for the view!" So let's do justice. Let's be the voice of justice when women have been abused by hurtful men, when the unborn and children have been abandoned, whenever the evil of white supremacy raises its ugly head, and when the imprisoned, the immigrant, and the poor are neglected. When war breaks out between nations or families, let's be the first to model the ways of peace.

GOD'S FUTURE

We work for peace and justice in the way of reconciliation today because we are people who believe Jesus is Lord and we are following him into a future where everything, including heaven and earth, are coming together. Not only have God and people been separated and divided, but God's space has been ripped apart from humanity's space. God created the heavens and the earth to exist in a beautiful harmony. In fact, God made the earth to be a temple where God could dwell. In the beginning God would walk with humanity "in the garden in the cool of the day" (Genesis 3:8). We chose to doubt God. We chose to pursue knowledge without God. We chose to try to reach God without God. A fissure was formed between heaven (God's space) and earth (our space) as a result of our stubborn ways. God's plan, when the time is right, is to "unite all things in him, things in heaven and things on earth" (Ephesians 1:10). We are following Jesus into this kind of future, not where we leave earth in order to go to heaven, but a future in which heaven comes to earth. This movement is the grand fulfillment of the prayer we pray day by day: *thy kingdom come, thy will be done on earth as it is in heaven.* When we pray for God's reign and rule to come on the earth, we are anticipating the day when heaven and earth are reunited and re-created into something new.

John the Revelator penned these words at the end of our story in the book of Revelation:

> Then I saw a new heaven and a new earth, for the first heaven and the first earth had passed away, and the sea was no more. And I saw the holy city, new Jerusalem, coming down out of heaven from God, prepared as a bride adorned for her husband. And I heard a loud voice from the throne saying, "Behold, the dwelling place of God is with man. He will dwell with them, and they will be his people, and God himself will be with them as their God. He will wipe away every tear from their eyes, and death shall be no more, neither shall there be mourning, nor crying, nor pain anymore, for the former things have passed away." (Revelation 21:1-4)

The movement recorded by John is not leaving the earth and going up to heaven, but heaven itself coming to earth. Why? Because God loves this place. God loves every part of his creation—the trees, the meadows of green grass, the sandy beaches, and the rocky, rugged mountains. Most importantly, God loves the creatures who bear his image, human beings of every nation, race, language, and tribe.

This picture of the future matters, because it becomes the goal which shapes what we do today. One way we describe this future is with the words "the age to come."[6] We live in the present evil age where things are often broken and out of sorts. Through our baptism we receive "eternal life," that is, the life of the age to come. In this way our baptism serves as a portal into the future where we experience the life of God's future. However, the present evil world remains among us. We live at the overlap of these two ages, one foot planted in the present age and the other foot planted in the age to come.

Jesus "gave himself for our sins to deliver us from the present evil age" (Galatians 1:4). He has delivered us from the age of darkness and destruction and delivered us to Mt. Zion, God's future, where nobody gets hurt or destroyed. We live in the tension of this in-between space where we live as kingdom citizens in this fallen world. Knowing exactly how to do justice in the world requires discernment from our local gathering, but we take our lead from the direction in which we are headed, from God's future where we are seated with Jesus, whom we are following.

GOD'S PLAN TO CHANGE THE WORLD

When I was a child, my mother kept her fine china in a cabinet in the dining room like most North American mothers. The collection of bowls, platters, plates, cups, and saucers were made of the finest materials, decorated with classy white flowers and leaves, and edged in platinum. Our particular set of china was "Grace Fine China, Concerto," made (ironically enough) in Japan. I remember being told once as a child that these were special dishes you use to serve a meal when important people come to your house. I suppose no one that important ever came to share a meal with us, because in the eighteen years of living in my parents' home, I don't ever remember using that china. Presidents Carter, Reagan, or Bush never came to our house for a meal, so the china remained housed in the china cabinet, put away for a special purpose, set aside and protected from the daily use of holding cereal and milk, peanut butter and jelly sandwiches, and fried pork chops. Our china was too exquisite, too elegant to be covered with ketchup and French fries. It was special and sacred. It was holy.

As followers of Jesus we are "a chosen race, a royal priesthood, a holy nation, a people for his own possession, that [we] may proclaim the excellencies of him who called [us] out of darkness into his marvelous light" (1 Peter 2:9). All of us who have come through the waters of baptism to follow Jesus into God's new world are a single chosen race, the chosen people of God, chosen for the mission of reflecting God's healing image into the world through acts of justice. We are special and sacred. We are holy. To be holy doesn't necessarily mean we are "religious," even though our religious practices form us and perfect us in holiness. To be holy, like my mother's fine china, means we are set apart for a special purpose. We are a royal priesthood, holy representatives sent into the world to make known the goodness of God and the way to true human flourishing. Unlike my mother's china, we are not reserved for the "important people." We are sent into every person's world.

As we read in the ancient *Epistle of Mathetes to Diognetus*, the mark of the people of God is "they are residents at home in their own countries, their behaviour there is more like that of transients; they take their full part as citizens, but they also submit to anything and everything as if they were aliens. For them, any foreign country is a motherland, and any motherland is a foreign country."[7] God breathes into his church and we come alive, but strangely so. The Spirit shapes us into a distinct people as we follow Jesus, and this distinctiveness and holiness is God's plan for changing the world. We don't gather together to try to devise a plan to change the world. We *are* that plan. The way we love God and one another, the way we love our neighbors and the weakest and most vulnerable around us, work together to form God's plan to change and heal his broken world.

We dwell in our own particular countries. We dwell in these countries, but only as sojourners. Our passports have been issued from heaven, so that we find our identity as the peculiar, set-apart, holy people of God. We share in all things in the communities where we live, but we endure ridicule and insults as strangers who belong to a multicultural family united in following Jesus. Our neighborhoods are filled with fear and anxiety, anger and angst, made exponentially worse by politicians drunk with power and blinded by dualistic good-guys-and-bad-guys kind of thinking. These fearmongers play on this anxiety and anger in order to garner votes. In light of the violence and fear, we as the people of God can be the soul in this maddening political body by resisting the spirit of our age, resisting the anger, the finger-pointing, and blame.

We can be the soul—the salt and light, if you will—in our local communities by living as the people of love and mercy. In the face of mistrust, we offer faith. In the face of despair, we offer hope. In the face of hate, we offer love. If we are willing to look remarkably different than the world as we love one another, then we have a chance, not to change the world, but to bear witness to the world of the alternative and life-giving way of Jesus. We do not change the world by our holiness; changing the world is not our task. We don't create some kind of mission, because God already has a mission in the world. According to Christopher Wright, "It is not so much the case that God has a mission for his church in the world but that God has a church for his mission in the world. Mission was not made for the church; the church was made for mission— God's mission."[8] This mission is the redemption of the world through King Jesus. Our mission is to follow Jesus and to love in such a way that people see King Jesus ruling and reigning over a kingdom of peace. Jesus is the Savior. He is changing the world. We are the ones who believe in Jesus and in his ways of reigning as King. We are the ones who follow the King wherever he leads.

discussion **questions**

1. Who were your heroes growing up? How did you honor them?

2. Who are your heroes today? How do you honor them?

3. How does war represent the brokenness of our world?

4. What are the key differences between justice as punishing lawbreakers and justice as setting right what's wrong in our world?

5. How has your background and upbringing shaped how you think about justice?

6. How do acts of justice prove we are disciples of Jesus?

7. What are the best ways to make disciples fit for God's mission?

8. Why does living at the overlap of the ages, between the present evil age and the future age to come, make doing justice so difficult?

9. What are some of the top needs for justice and reconciliation you see in our world?

10. What can you do to be an instrument of peace in your family, neighborhood, and church?

Appendix

A MORNING PRAYER LITURGY

Opening Address

Father God, creator of heaven and earth,
God of Abraham, Isaac, and Jacob,
God of Israel,
God and Father of our Lord and Savior Jesus Christ,
    true and living God who is Father, Son, and Holy Spirit,
    have mercy and hear my prayer.

First Prayers

O Lord, open our lips,
and our mouths shall proclaim your praise.
Glory to the Father, and to the Son, and to the Holy Spirit:
    as it was in the beginning, is now, and will be forever.
    Amen. Hallelujah.
O God, make speed to save us. O Lord, make haste to help us.

Glory to the Father, and to the Son, and to the Holy Spirit:
as it was in the beginning, is now, and will be forever.
Amen. Hallelujah.

The Jesus Prayer

Lord Jesus Christ, Son of God, have mercy on me.

Confession of Sin

Most merciful God,
  we confess that we have sinned against you
  in thought, word, and deed
  by what we have done,
  and by what we have left undone.
We have not loved you with our whole heart;
  we have not loved our neighbors as ourselves.
We are truly sorry and we humbly repent.
For the sake of your Son Jesus Christ,
  have mercy on us and forgive us,
  that we may delight in your will
  and walk in your ways,
  to the glory of your name. Amen.

Psalm for the Day

(Corresponding to the day of the year)

Scripture Reading

(Old Testament, Epistle, and Gospel reading from the Daily
  Office Lectionary)

Apostles' Creed

I believe in God, the Father almighty,
  creator of heaven and earth.
I believe in Jesus Christ, his only Son, our Lord.

He was conceived by the power of the Holy Spirit
  and born of the Virgin Mary.
He suffered under Pontius Pilate,
  was crucified, died, and was buried.
He descended to the dead.
On the third day he rose again.
He ascended into heaven,
  and is seated at the right of the Father.
He will come again to judge the living and the dead.
I believe in the Holy Spirit,
  the holy catholic Church,
  the communion of the saints,
  the forgiveness of sins,
  the resurrection of the body,
  and the life everlasting. Amen.

Prayer for the Week
(Contemporary Collect from *The Book of Common Prayer*)

The Lord's Prayer
Our Father, who art in heaven,
  hallowed be thy name,
  thy kingdom come,
  thy will be done,
  on earth as it is in heaven.
Give us this day our daily bread.
And forgive us our trespasses,
  as we forgive those who trespass against us.
And lead us not into temptation,
  but deliver us from evil.
For thine is the kingdom, and the power, and the glory, for ever.
  Amen.

Prayer for Family

Lord I pray that you bless (*name each family member by name*).
Protect them and keep them safe.
Lead them in the way of life everlasting.

Petition and Intercession

(*Making our needs known and praying for others*)

Contemplation

(*Sitting with Jesus in silence*)

Prayer to the Crucified Christ

Lord Jesus, you stretched out your arms of love upon the hard
wood of the cross that everyone might come within the reach
of your saving embrace. So clothe us in your Spirit that we,
reaching forth our hands in love, may bring those who do not
know you to the knowledge and love of you, for the honor of
your name. Amen.

Prayer of St. Francis

Lord, make me an instrument of your peace:
 where there is hatred, let me sow love;
 where there is injury, pardon;
 where there is doubt, faith;
 where there is despair, hope;
 where there is darkness, light;
 where there is sadness, joy.
O divine Master, grant that I may not so much seek
 to be consoled as to console,
 to be understood as to understand,
 to be loved as to love.
For it is in giving that we receive,
 it is in pardoning that we are pardoned,

and it is in dying that we are born to eternal life.
Amen.

Prayer for Mercy
Lord, have mercy.
Christ, have mercy.
Lord, have mercy.

Confession of the Mystery
Christ has died.
Christ is risen.
Christ will come again.

Jesus Prayer
Lord Jesus Christ, Son of God, have mercy on me.
In the name of the Father, Son, and Holy Spirit,
Amen.

This morning prayer liturgy offers a structure for prayer that takes some time to learn, but once you memorize the structure you will find your life of prayer flourish. The Opening Address, First Prayers, Jesus Prayer, and Confession of Sin are the same every morning. Read them aloud, slowly at first, but work on committing them to memory. Once memorized, continue to pray the liturgy slowly and purposefully. The Psalm for the Day corresponds to the day of the year. On day 1 (January 1), read aloud Psalm 1 as a prayer. On day 45 pray Psalm 45, and so on. When you reach day 151, start over with Psalm 1 and continue through day 300. On day 301, start over again with Psalm 1 until day 365, when you pray Psalm 65.

This liturgy of prayer draws heavily upon the Anglican and Episcopal prayer book *The Book of Common Prayer*.[1]

This prayer book is a gift to the English-speaking world from the English Reformation of the sixteenth century. It has been edited numerous times and the 1979 edition I use has become a helpful addition to my prayer life. While large sections of this prayer book are specifically for Anglican worship, many of the prayers and the original translation of the Psalms are a real treasure. If *The Book of Common Prayer* is unfamiliar to you, I'd recommend *Our Common Prayer: A Field Guide to the Book of Common Prayer* by Winfield Bevins.[2] This little book is a great introduction to the common prayer tradition and it also has a number of the prayers from *The Book of Common Prayer* in it.

The Scripture readings in the morning prayer liturgy are from the Old Testament, Epistles, and Gospels for each day and can be found in the Daily Office Lectionary in the back of *The Book of Common Prayer,* or online on various websites and mobile phone apps.[3] The Apostles' Creed is read aloud as prayer, and as with the beginning section of the liturgy, should also be committed to memory as you grow more familiar with it. The Prayer for the Week is drawn from the traditional "collect" found in *The Book of Common Prayer*.[4] This prayer is offered as a part of worship in liturgical churches and corresponds to the liturgical calendar which can be found in the Revised Common Lectionary, located online in various places.[5] For example, on the first Sunday of Advent, normally the first Sunday in December, we offer the "collect," or prayer, for the first Sunday in Advent. The Lord's Prayer can be committed to memory.

The Prayer for Family is a daily prayer I pray for each of my immediate family members. Feel free to pray for your family as you see fit. The Petition and Intercession part is where you are invited to pray from your heart, to make known the requests you have for yourself or others. This section of prayer can be different every day. It's a matter of what things or which people you want to pray for. Contemplation is sitting quietly in the presence of Jesus. This prayer is offered without words in silence. Be open to the surprising work of the Holy Spirit here. Embrace the silence. Focus your thoughts by repeating the Jesus Prayer in your mind or focus on your breathing if necessary.

As we come out of silence, pray the Prayer to the Crucified Christ, the Prayer of St. Francis, the Prayer for Mercy, the Confession of the Mystery, and the Jesus Prayer. Just like with the Opening Prayer, read these prayers aloud slowly and work to memorize them. Once you have committed them to memory continue to pray them slowly and purposefully, preparing yourself to enter into your day. I adapted this from Brian Zahnd's "Liturgy for Morning Prayer."[6] Feel free to adapt my liturgy to fit the traditions of your church or your own practice of prayer. The important thing is to find opening and closing prayers you memorize, and to include Scripture readings, the creed, and moments of silence.

Notes

INTRODUCTION

1. Stanley Hauerwas, *Approaching the End: Eschatological Reflections on Church, Politics, and Life* (Grand Rapids, MI: Eerdmans, 2013), 67.
2. Dallas Willard, *The Divine Conspiracy: Rediscovering Our Hidden Life in God* (New York: HarperCollins, 1998), 301.

CHAPTER 1

1. By "evangelical" I am referring to Christians who are marked by the following characteristics: (1) a high value for the authority of Scripture; (2) a desire to make the gospel known to those who are not Christians; (3) belief in the centrality of the death of Jesus for the salvation of humanity and the redemption of

the world; and (4) belief in the necessity of a personal experience of conversion.

2. Maxwell Staniforth, trans., *Early Christian Writings* (New York: Penguin Books, 1987), 191.

3. See Psalm 5:8; 18:21; 25:4, 8-9; 44:18; 119:1-3; 128:1-2; 138:4-5.

4. Eugene Peterson, *The Jesus Way* (Grand Rapids, MI: Eerdmans, 2007), 4.

CHAPTER 2

1. N. T. Wright, *Simply Good News* (San Francisco: HarperOne, 2017), 12–13.

2. Bruxy Cavey, *Reunion: The Good News of Jesus for Seekers, Saints, and Sinners* (Harrisonburg, VA: Herald Press, 2017), 52.

CHAPTER 3

1. As quoted by Leo G. Cox, "John Wesley's Concept of Sin," *The Journal of the Evangelical Theological Society 5*, no. 1 (Winter, 1962): 20.

2. John Wesley, "On Sin in Believers," in *The Works of John Wesley: Volume 1*, ed. Albert Outler (Nashville, TN: Abingdon, 1984), 320.

3. Thomas Merton, *No Man Is an Island* (San Diego: Harcourt, 1955; reprint, New York: Barnes & Noble, 2003), 18.

4. Sean Palmer, *Unarmed Empire* (Eugene, OR: Cascade Books, 2017), 109.

5. This quote has been attributed to C.S. Lewis, but it does not appear in any of his writings. Lewis did write: "Do not imagine that if you meet a really humble man

he will be what most people call 'humble' nowadays: he will not be a sort of greasy, smarmy person, who is always telling you that, of course, he is nobody. Probably all you will think about him is that he seemed a cheerful, intelligent chap who took a real interest in what you said to him. If you do dislike him it will be because you feel a little envious of anyone who seems to enjoy life so easily. He will not be thinking about humility: he will not be thinking about himself at all." C. S. Lewis, *Mere Christianity* (New York: Macmillan Publishing, 1960), 114.

6. Staniforth, *Early Christian Writings*, 144–45.
7. James M. Washington, ed., *A Testament of Hope: The Essential Writings and Speeches* (New York: HarperOne, 2003), 257.

CHAPTER 4

1. N. T. Wright, *The Resurrection of the Son of God* (Minneapolis, MN: Fortress, 2003), 237.
2. "Selected Liturgical Hymns," Orthodox Church in America, accessed April 15, 2018, oca.org/orthodoxy/prayers/selected-liturgical-hymns.
3. See Micah 4:2.
4. I am indebted to the work of fellow staff members at Word of Life Church in St. Joseph for their input in specifying the language of these four practices. Jacob and Megan Taylor, Paul Tassler, Mardi Solomon, and Stan Shaver all worked with me on our "focus team" to develop the final version of these practices.
5. John Delaney, trans., *The Practice of the Presence of God* (New York: Image Books, 1977), 95.

CHAPTER 5

1. As quoted by Leo J. O'Donovan, *Finding God in All Things*, ed. Mark Bosco and David Stagaman (New York: Fordham, 2007), 131.

2. Kallistos Ware describes the love of God as unceasing movement, "The Christian God is not just a unit but a union, not just unity but community. There is in God something analogous to 'society.' He is not a single person, loving himself alone, not a self-contained monad or 'The One.' He is triunity: three equal persons, each one dwelling in the other two by virtue of an unceasing movement of mutual love." Kallistos Ware, *The Orthodox Way* (Crestwood, NY: St. Vladimir's Seminary, 1979), 27.

3. Philip Schaff, *History of the Christian Church*, vol. 3 (Peabody, MA: Hendrickson, 1996), 673.

4. Gregory of Nazianzus, *Orations 40:41*. As quoted by Thomas Oden, *The Living God* (San Francisco: Harper & Row, 1987), 216.

5. Darrell Johnson, *Experiencing the Trinity* (Vancouver, BC: Regent College, 2002), 61.

6. Colin Gunton, *The Christian Faith* (Malden, MA: Blackwell Publishers, 2002), 190.

7. Brad Jersak, *A More Christlike God* (Pasadena, CA: Plain Truth Ministries, 2015), 199.

8. Robert Hemfelt, Frank Minirth, Paul Meier, *Love Is a Choice* (Nashville, TN: Thomas Nelson, 1989), 5.

9. Henry Cloud and John Townsend, *Boundaries* (Grand Rapids, MI: Zondervan, 1993), 31.

10. Gunton, *The Christian Faith*, 188.

CHAPTER 6

1. N. T. Wright, *After You Believe* (New York: Harper-Collins, 2010), 158.
2. Wright, *After You Believe*, 158.
3. Mark Noll, *The Scandal of the Evangelical Mind* (Grand Rapids, MI: Eerdmans, 1994), 3.
4. Dallas Willard, *Renovation of the Heart* (Colorado Springs, CO: NavPress, 2002), 106.

CHAPTER 7

1. "Christians: More like Jesus or Pharisees?," Barna, June 3, 2013, www.barna.com/research/christians-more-like-jesus-or-pharisees/.
2. Thomas à Kempis, *The Imitation of Christ*, reprint, trans. William C. Creasy (Notre Dame, IN: Ave Maria Press, 2017), 25.
3. Willard, *Renovation of the Heart*, 87.
4. John Ortberg, et. al., *Growth: Training vs. Trying* (Grand Rapids, MI: Zondervan, 2000), 4.

CHAPTER 8

1. Dietrich Bonhoeffer, *Life Together* (New York: Harper & Row, 1954; reprint, San Francisco: HarperOne, 2009), 27.
2. We believe in one church even though we worship in different buildings and express our faith in different traditions and denominations. This one church is holy, set apart for God's mission on the earth. The church is "catholic" in that it is universal. Furthermore, the church is "apostolic," in that it is shaped by the

teachings of the apostles (Acts 2:42) which became the
New Testament.

3. Stanley Hauerwas and William H. Willimon, *Resident
    Aliens: A Provocative Christian Assessment of Culture
    and Ministry for People Who Know That Something
    Is Wrong* (Nashville, TN: Abingdon, 1989), 83.

CHAPTER 9

1. Alan Kreider, *The Patient Ferment of the Early Church:
    The Improbable Rise of Christianity in the Roman
    Empire* (Grand Rapids, MI: Eerdmans, 2011), 40. See
    also James K. A. Smith, who adds, "*Habitus* is a kind
    of embodied tradition . . . it is something that comes
    to me, from outside me, conditioning and enabling my
    constitution of the world." James K.A. Smith, *Imagin-
    ing the Kingdom* (Grand Rapids, MI: Baker Academic
    2013), 81.

2. Aristotle, *The Nicomachean Ethics*, trans. David Ross
    (Oxford: Oxford University Press, 2009), 23.

3. This concept was adapted from "The Four Stages
    for Learning Any New Skill" developed by Gordon
    Training International. www.gordontraining.com/free-
    workplace-articles/learning-a-new-skill-is-easier-said-
    than-done/.

4. Peter Scazzero, *Emotionally Healthy Spirituality,
    Updated Edition* (Grand Rapids, MI: Zondervan,
    2017), 190.

5. Jaroslav Pelikan, *The Vindication of Tradition: The
    1983 Jefferson Lecture in the Humanities* (New
    Haven, CT: Yale University Press, 1986), 65.

6. Brian Zahnd, *Water to Wine: Some of My Story* (St. Joseph, MO: Spello Press, 2016), 89.

7. Zahnd, *Water to Wine*, 74.

8. Stuart Murray, *The Naked Anabaptist: Fifth Anniversary Edition* (Harrisonburg, VA: Herald Press, 2015), 73.

9. As quoted by Daniel B. Clendenin, *Eastern Orthodox Theology: A Contemporary Reader* (Grand Rapids, MI: Baker Academic: 2003), 99.

10. See Richard Foster's classic work *Celebration of Discipline* for a full description of the classic habits or disciplines of the faith including: meditation, fasting, study, simplicity, solitude, submission, service, and others. Richard J. Foster, *Celebration of Discipline, Special Anniversary Edition: The Path to Spiritual Growth* (New York: HarperOne, 2018).

11. Gordon T. Smith, *Evangelical, Sacramental, and Pentecostal: Why the Church Should Be All Three* (Downers Grove, IL: IVP Academic, 2017), 83.

12. See Glenn Packiam, *Blessed Broken Given: How Your Story Becomes Sacred in the Hands of Jesus* (Colorado Springs, CO: Waterbook, 2019). I am thankful for Glenn's insightful observation on communion as not only the centerpiece of Christian worship but also the vision of the church as the blessed, broken, and given people.

CHAPTER 10

1. To get a full-scale picture of the Vietnam War see Ken Burns and Lynn Novick, *The Vietnam War* (2017; Walpole, NH: Florentine Films, 2017), DVD.

2. www.nps.gov/mlkm/learn/quotations.htm.
3. Christopher Wright, *The Mission of God: Unlocking the Bible's Grand Narrative* (Grand Rapids, MI: IVP Academic, 2006), 67.
4. David Fitch, *Faithful Presence: Seven Disciplines That Shape the Church for Mission* (Downers Grove, IL: InterVarsity, 2016), 71–72.
5. N. T. Wright, *The Day the Revolution Began: Reconsidering the Meaning of Jesus's Crucifixion* (San Francisco: HarperOne, 2016), 365.
6. See Mark 10:30; Luke 18:30; 1 Corinthians 10:11; Ephesians 1:21; Hebrews 6:5.
7. Maxwell Staniforth, trans., *Early Christian Writings* (New York, Penguin Books, 1987), 144–45.
8. Wright, *The Mission of God*, 63.

APPENDIX

1. *1979 Book of Common Prayer* (New York: Oxford University Press, 2008).
2. Winfield Bevins, *Our Common Prayer: A Field Guide to the Book of Common Prayer* (Charleston, SC: Simeon Press, 2013).
3. The Daily Office Lectionary is found in the *1979 Book of Common Prayer*, 936–95. It is a two-year system. Year 1 begins on the first Sunday of Advent during the Advent season before odd-numbered years, and Year 2 begins during Advent before even-numbered years. So on the first Sunday of Advent in 2018 we began Year 1, because 2019 is an odd-numbered year. You can also access *The Book of Common Prayer* online at www.bcponline.org.

4. "Collects: Contemporary," *1979 Book of Common Prayer*, 211–36.

5. For example, at lectionary.library.vanderbilt.edu.

6. Zahnd, *Water to Wine*, 80–89.

The Author

Derek Vreeland is the discipleship pastor at Word of Life Church in St. Joseph, Missouri, where he leads small groups and discipleship ministries and serves on the pastoral leadership team along with Brian and Peri Zahnd. Vreeland is a regular contributor at Missio Alliance, and his work has been published by *Outreach*. The author of several books, Vreeland has degrees from Missouri Western State University, Oral Roberts University, and Asbury Theological Seminary. He and his wife, Jenni, have three sons.